I AM Rooted!

This Journal Belongs To:

....

Date:

....

This book is lovingly dedicated to the One whose love and Word
has drawn me since childhood. Your kindness and tender mercy has
preserved me in more ways than I can count; to Jesus my King.
And to my family and friends... thank you for your constant
encouragement, support, and prayers throughout this journey.

A NOTE TO PARENTS

In the spring of 2017, I set out to uproot five trees that my husband and I had planted in our backyard two years prior. Out of all of the trees planted only one was healthy and growing. Standing at almost triple the height of the other four, this tree was flourishing and blooming. A hard shove against its trunk proved that it wasn't going anywhere. This tree was solid and unmovable because it had developed a healthy root system.

However, when I grabbed each of the other trees by their trunks I was surprised at how easily they came out of the soil. Even though they all had leaves their roots were weak and shallow, making them easier to shift.

It dawned on me that the first tree illustrated the kind of spiritual root system I wanted my kids to have. I wanted them to be unmovable, strong, rooted in the truth of God's Word, and overflowing with thankfulness (Colossians 2:7). I wanted kids who were spiritually flourishing in every season of life particularly when things were hard.

These desires of mine turned into the devotional and gratitude journal you are holding.

Through this journal your kid will begin to develop solid Biblical roots as they discover the countless ways God loves them, helps them, and guides them in their everyday lives. Raising Biblically rooted kids begins with getting them into God's Word every day!

This is sure to be a life-giving process as you see your kid grow solid Biblical roots and the tremendous fruit that results when we stay connected to the Lord through His Word and prayer.

In the service of the King,
Amanda Lee

INSIDE THIS JOURNAL YOU WILL FIND:

Interactive daily devotionals + fun doodle and journal prompts

Each week your kid will learn a new important concept about God. These devotions are packed with Scripture and also include fun and interactive doodle and journal prompts to help them relate to the devotion and remember it!

Daily and monthly mood trackers

Each day will finish with a fun dog mood tracker. After coloring their mood for the day, your kid will be prompted to flip to a monthly mood tracker chart and fill it in. This chart is a wonderful tool to keep track of their emotional health that month.

Daily thankfulness + prayer prompts

Solid Biblical roots develop when our kids learn how to practice daily thankfulness and prayer. Every day they will end their devotional time by writing one thing they are thankful for and what they are praying for that day. At the end of the week or month, they can look back on their journal and see how God has answered their prayers.

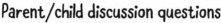

Parent/child discussion questions

At the end of the week, enjoy some quality time with your kid as you go through discussion questions about what they learned.

Scripture writing challenges

Writing down Scripture helps the brain remember it! At the end of each week your kid will be challenged to write out that week's key Bible verse. They can also choose to memorize it!

6

FREQUENTLY ASKED QUESTIONS:

"What age is this journal for?"

I Am Rooted! is designed for ages 9-12 but can also be used by younger kids with assistance. It is designed to be fun and interactive so younger and older kids alike will enjoy doodling and writing what they are learning, what they are thankful for, and what they are praying for.

"Is this journal meant to be completed independently?"

I Am Rooted! is designed to be easy to follow and can be completed by your kid independently. Discussion questions at the end of the week will allow you to participate in what they learned that week.

"How many weeks are covered in this journal?"

I Am Rooted! is broken into 12 weeks covering 3 foundational truths: God Loves, God Helps, and God Guides. Each week is made up of 5 days of devotionals with each day building on the concept being taught.

"How long does each day take to complete?"

Each day is designed to take anywhere from 5-15 minutes to complete.

"What kinds of coloring tools should my kid use?"

There are plenty of opportunities for your kid to color in their journal! To prevent bleeding from markers it is a good idea to test your kids' markers on the pages at the back of the book. Pencil crayons and crayons can also be used and may work better than markers.

ADDITIONAL TIPS:

It will be helpful for your kid to bookmark their monthly mood tracker chart with a sticky note. This will save them the hassle of having to find it every day. **NOTE: Each month has it's own mood tracker chart so make sure they are marking the correct one!** These can be found at the end of each chapter and can be easily located using the Table of Contents.

If your kid needs extra journal space additional journal pages can be found at the back of the book.

I AM Rooted!

Chapter
1. GOD LOVES

Chapter
2. GOD HELPS

Chapter
3. GOD GUIDES

Chapter One
GOD LOVES

"And may you have the power to understand, as all God's people should, how wide, how long, how high, and how deep his love is."

Ephesians 3:18 (NLT)

Week One

BREAKING RECORDS

(How big is God's love?)

Today is: (Color the day of the week)

S M T W T F S

DAY ONE

PLANTING A SEED

Breaking Records
(How big is God's love?)

"And may you have the power to understand, as all God's people should, how wide, how long, how high, and how deep his love is."
Ephesians 3:18 (NLT)

Every year, a book of world records is published containing records on almost anything you can imagine. There is a world record for the widest river, the tallest waterfall, the largest toy gun, the longest train set, the largest marker, the widest tongue, and even the deepest scuba dive by a dog!

Pretty much anything you can imagine can be measured and has a world record. People who wish to submit a world record must follow a specific standard of record keeping based on measurement.

Imagine you were to trying to figure out the world record for love, what do you think you would find? Is there a way to measure how much God loves us?

Read:
"Your unfailing love, O Lord, is as vast as the heavens; your faithfulness reaches beyond the clouds. Your righteousness is like the mighty mountains, your justice like the ocean depths. You care for people and animals alike, O Lord. How precious is your unfailing love, O God! All humanity finds shelter in the shadow of your wings."
Psalm 36:5-7 (NLT)

Psalm 36 tells us that God's love reaches all the way to the heavens. God's love is higher than the tallest waterfall, longer than the longest train set, wider than any river, and deeper than any ocean on our planet.

The Bible says that God knows everything about us and He sees the deepest parts of our hearts. God also showed His love for us by giving us His son Jesus as a way to spend eternity with Him.

Now that's a measurement of love you won't find in any record book!

14

Use this space to journal. You can write about what you learned today, your worries, your thoughts, or your prayers.

....

....

....

....

....

....

Finishing Off

God, today I am feeling... (Circle or color)

Happy

Blessed

Anxious

Sad

Angry

I feel this way because ....

....

Today I am thankful for ....

Today I am praying for ....

....

Go to page 69 and fill in your "Monthly Mood Tracker" chart.

WEEK ONE
Breaking
Records

Today is: (Color the day of the week)

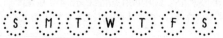

S M T W T F S

DAY TWO

WATERING FOR GROWTH

Have you ever wondered if God could see you? If you have you are not alone. After all, it can be easy to think that because we can't see God, He can't see us. But is that true? What does the Bible say about how God sees us?

Read:

"O Lord, you have examined my heart and know everything about me. You know when I sit down or stand up. You know my thoughts even when I'm far away. You see me when I travel and when I rest at home. You know everything I do."

Psalm 139:1-3 (NLT)

Circle the word **everything**. (Hint: there are 2)

God tells us that He knows absolutely everything about us! He knows our thoughts and our hearts. He sees us when we get up in the morning, when we struggle with a friend, when we have a bad day, and even when we lay awake at night. He sees the deepest parts of our hearts—our joys, triumphs, fears, and anxieties. God has the ability to know us far better than any human ever could.

Read:

"You watched me as I was being formed in utter seclusion, as I was woven together in the dark of the womb. You saw me before I was born. Every day of my life was recorded in your book. Every moment was laid out before a single day had passed."

Psalm 139:15-16 (NLT)

Circle the phrase **saw me before I was born.**

The love of a parent is a powerful thing. From the time they learned you were on the way your parents love for you began to grow. The Bible tells us that God's love for us began even before our parents knew we existed!

God already decided every single day you would live down to each and every minute of your life. God knows you better than anyone in this entire world. He knew you and loved you even before you were born.

Read:

"And the very hairs on your head are all numbered."

Matthew 10:30 (NLT)

Just in case you were still not convinced, God also tells us that He sees and knows the number of every single hair on our head.

Think about everything you have learned today. Do you think it is possible for God to see you and love you even though you can't see Him?

16

CHAPTER ONE, WEEK ONE | BREAKING RECORDS

Yesterday my mom and I were looking through old baby albums from when I was really small. On one of the pages she recorded special moments she wanted to remember like when I first walked, when I first talked, or when I first ate solid food. (I guess I didn't like peas very much!) It was really cool to look at the pictures and read her notes. **It made me feel loved** to know that she kept a record of my special moments. I think it is amazing that before I was even born God already planned and wrote every single day of my life in His book. I can't believe He loves me that much.

What is one thing you learned today that you want to remember?

....

....

....

Finishing Off

God, today I am feeling... (Circle or color)

Happy

Blessed

Anxious

Sad

Angry

I feel this way because ....

....

Today I am thankful for ....

Today I am praying for ....

....

17

Go to page 69 and fill in your "Monthly Mood Tracker" chart.

WEEK ONE
Breaking
Records

Today is: (Color the day of the week)

S M T W T F S

DAY THREE

GROWING ROOTS

Love is a word we use a lot. Think about the word love and how often you use it. Have you ever tasted a gooey slice of pizza and said, "This is so good, I love it!"? Or have you ever received a new gadget or toy for Christmas and shrieked, "Thank you so much, I LOVE it!"? Most of us use the word love to describe how we feel about a variety of things. But have you noticed how the things you once loved can quickly lose their appeal? Our interests or tastes can change so often. Things we once loved can become boring and soon we are onto the next thing.

Read:

"Long ago the Lord said to Israel: 'I have loved you, my people, with an everlasting love. With unfailing love I have drawn you to myself.'"
Jeremiah 31:3 (NLT)

Circle or underline the phrases **everlasting love** and **unfailing love**.

How is God's love different from our love for things? Does God's love ever run out? Does it ever change?

Journal your thoughts below.

....

....

God's love is everlasting and unfailing. How God feels about us never ever changes. In fact, the Bible tells us that God loves us so much that He thinks about us constantly.

Read:

"How precious are your thoughts about me, O God. They cannot be numbered! I can't even count them; they outnumber the grains of sand! And when I wake up, you are still with me!"
Psalm 139:17-18 (NLT)

Isn't it amazing that the God of the universe is thinking about you all the time?

Have you ever sank your toes into the warm sand on a beach? If so, think about each individual tiny grain of sand. Now imagine every single grain of sand on every single beach in the entire world. God's thoughts towards us are even more still!

Isn't God's love amazing? God tells us that unlike our definition of love; His love never changes.

18

Doodle yourself on a beach. God's thoughts about you are more than every grain of sand.

Finishing Off

God, today I am feeling... (Circle or color)

Happy   **Blessed**   **Anxious**   **Sad**   **Angry**

I feel this way because ....

....

Today I am thankful for ....

Today I am praying for ....

....

Go to page 69 and fill in your "Monthly Mood Tracker" chart.

Today is: (Color the day of the week)

(S) (M) (T) (W) (T) (F) (S)

DAY FOUR

HARVESTING THE FRUIT

God sees us and He loves us! Because He loves us He promises to take care of our needs.
We all have two kinds of needs: physical and spiritual. Both are important to God but did you know that our spiritual needs are most important?

Can you think of an example of a spiritual need? Write it below.

....

God cares about His children and He promises to help us have enough to eat, clothing, safety, and a place to live. God invites us to trust Him for **every need** we have and He promises to provide.

Read:
"And my God will supply every need of yours according to his riches in glory in Christ Jesus."
Philippians 4:19 (ESV)

Circle the phrase **God will supply every need of yours.**

What needs are you trusting God to provide for you or your family right now?

....

Have you ever thought about the difference between a need and a want? What do you think is the difference?

....

....

Here's a fact: Everyone has spiritual needs that money can't buy. Jesus came to provide for our spiritual needs like forgiveness, peace, and eternal life just to name a few!

Read:
"For this is how God loved the world: He gave his one and only Son, so that everyone who believes in him will not perish but have eternal life."
John 3:16 (NLT)

You can skip ahead to Page 175 for more about how Jesus wants to meet our spiritual needs.

20

Write about a time you saw God meet your needs or the needs of your family. What happened?

....

....

....

....

....

....

....

....

Finishing Off

God, today I am feeling... (Circle or color)

Happy	Blessed	Anxious	Sad	Angry

I feel this way because ....

....

Today I am thankful for ....

Today I am praying for ....

....

Go to page 69 and fill in your "Monthly Mood Tracker" chart.

WEEK ONE
Breaking Records

Today is: *(Color the day of the week)*

S M T W T F S

DAY FIVE

REVIEW AND DISCUSS

This week you learned that God sees you and loves you even if you can't see Him. If you could see God face-to-face what is one question you would ask Him?

....

....

....

....

....

God's love is higher than the tallest waterfall, longer than the longest train set, wider than any river, and deeper than any ocean on our planet. Do you think it is possible for His love for you to run out? Why or why not? (Hint: Read Romans 8:39 to find the answer.)

....

....

....

Go back through days 1-4 and look at what you have been praying for. How have you seen God answer your prayers this week?

....

....

....

22

Scripture Writing Challenge

Rewrite:
"Your unfailing love, O Lord, is as vast as the heavens; your faithfulness reaches beyond the clouds.
Your righteousness is like the mighty mountains, your justice like the ocean depths."
Psalm 36:5 (NLT)

....

....

....

....

Finishing Off

God, today I am feeling... (Circle or color)

Happy **Blessed** **Anxious** **Sad** **Angry**

I feel this way because ....

....

Today I am thankful for ....

Today I am praying for ....

....

Go to page 69 and fill in your "Monthly Mood Tracker" chart.

Discussion Questions

• Week One •

Pick one or more questions to discuss with your parents.

Kids ask your parents:

- How is God's love for me different than your love for me?
- In what ways have you seen God provide for our family?
- Has God ever provided for you in a big way? What was it?

Parents ask your kids:

- What did you learn about God's love this week?
- Who do you think knows you the best?
- What physical and spiritual needs does God give you and me?
- What is the difference between a need and a want?
- How can I pray for you this week?

Family Prayer Requests:

....

....

....

....

Doodles

Use this empty space to draw or doodle!

Week Two

A FISH OUT OF WATER

(Where do I belong?)

Today is: (Color the day of the week)

(S) (M) (T) (W) (T) (F) (S)

DAY ONE

PLANTING A SEED

A Fish Out of Water
(Where do I belong?)

> "The patriarchs became jealous of Joseph and sold him
> into Egypt. Yet God was with him."
> Acts 7:9 (NASB)

Sweaty palms. Heart racing. Butterflies in your tummy. Maybe you have felt one or more of these as you walk the hallways of a brand new school or church. Maybe you just joined a team and everyone knows one another and you feel left out. Are you the only Christian in your class and are constantly being reminded of how different you feel from the kids around you? A fish out of water or a square peg in a round hole—both of these must feel out of place like they don't belong where they are.

Have you ever been in a situation where you felt alone or out of place?

There is one man in the Bible who can relate to how you feel. One of 11 brothers from the tribe of Jacob, Joseph was a man who served the one and only God. He was raised to know God's Word and to lead a life that honored the Lord. His life and family centered around the Bible and serving God.

But one day Joseph found himself in very different waters than what he was used to back in Canaan. Sold into slavery by his jealous brothers, he suddenly felt alone in a land full of strange pagan rituals and false gods that went against everything he was taught.

Feeling like we don't belong can cause us to really question who we are. It must have been hard for Joseph to be in Egypt where he felt so out of place. The only thing that comforted Joseph was the reminder that God knew him and that He had a plan for him. Even in a strange place Joseph never forgot about God and how much God loved him. No matter how strange it felt to be in Egypt, Joseph always remembered that he belonged to God.

Knowing his true belonging helped Joseph succeed in Egypt. This week we will learn what our true belonging is and how we can also succeed even when we feel alone and out of place.

Use this space to journal. You can write about what you learned today, your worries, your thoughts, or your prayers.

....

....

....

....

....

....

....

....

....

Finishing Off

God, today I am feeling... *(Circle or color)*

Happy   **Blessed**   **Anxious**   **Sad**   **Angry**

I feel this way because ....

....

Today I am thankful for ....

Today I am praying for ....

....

Go to page 69 and fill in your "Monthly Mood Tracker" chart.

WEEK TWO
A Fish Out of Water

Today is: (Color the day of the week)

(S) (M) (T) (W) (T) (F) (S)

DAY TWO

WATERING FOR GROWTH

Read:
"See how very much our Father loves us, for he calls us his children, and that is what we are!"
1 John 3:1 (NLT)

and

"And, I will be a Father to you, and you will be my sons and daughters, says the Lord Almighty."
2 Corinthians 6:18 (NLT)

If God is our Father then who are we to Him? Look at the first verse.

He calls us His ....

If we are God's children that means that we not only belong to an earthly family but we also belong to another family—we belong to God's family.

"But you are a chosen people, a royal priesthood, a holy nation, God's special possession, that you may declare the praises of him who called you out of darkness into his wonderful light."
1 Peter 2:9 (NIV)

Circle the word **chosen**. What is your favorite sport or game? Is it soccer, baseball, basketball, or even tag? Have you ever known the feelings of embarrassment and hurt that come from being picked last for a team? Maybe you aren't very athletic and you often find yourself being the kid that no one wants to pick. Rejection from those around us can be very hurtful. It can be upsetting to be left out or feel like you are not wanted.

Read:
"You have been set apart as holy to the Lord your God, and he has chosen you from all the nations of the earth to be his own special treasure."
Deuteronomy 14:2 (NLT)

Circle the word **chosen** and the phrase **his own special treasure**.

The Bible tells us that before God even made the world, He loved us and chose us. Before we were even born God decided to adopt us into His own family. He values you and loves you so much that He calls you His special treasure.

When you feel the pain and hurt of being rejected don't forget that you have a Heavenly Father who wants you, values you, and loves you beyond words.

30

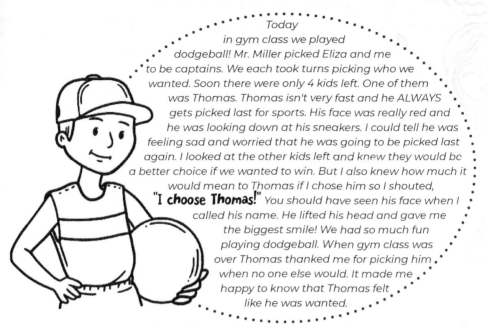

Today in gym class we played dodgeball! Mr. Miller picked Eliza and me to be captains. We each took turns picking who we wanted. Soon there were only 4 kids left. One of them was Thomas. Thomas isn't very fast and he ALWAYS gets picked last for sports. His face was really red and he was looking down at his sneakers. I could tell he was feeling sad and worried that he was going to be picked last again. I looked at the other kids left and knew they would be a better choice if we wanted to win. But I also knew how much it would mean to Thomas if I chose him so I shouted, **"I choose Thomas!"** *You should have seen his face when I called his name. He lifted his head and gave me the biggest smile! We had so much fun playing dodgeball. When gym class was over Thomas thanked me for picking him when no one else would. It made me happy to know that Thomas felt like he was wanted.*

Have you ever felt like Thomas? How does it make you feel to know that God has picked you to be part of His family?

....

Finishing Off

God, today I am feeling... (Circle or color)

Happy

Blessed

Anxious

Sad

Angry

I feel this way because ....

....

Today I am thankful for ....

Today I am praying for ....

....

Go to page 69 and fill in your "Monthly Mood Tracker" chart.

WEEK TWO
A Fish Out of Water

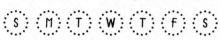

Today is: (Color the day of the week)

(S) (M) (T) (W) (T) (F) (S)

DAY THREE

GROWING ROOTS

Yesterday we learned that God picked us to be part of His family. Today we are going to learn about our friendship with God.

Read:

"I no longer call you slaves, because a master doesn't confide in his slaves. Now you are my friends, since I have told you everything the Father told me."

John 15:15 (NLT)

Did you know that God calls us His friends? Do you have a good friend? Write their name below.

....

What makes your friendship so awesome?

....

....

Sometimes it can be hard to find good friendships. Do you struggle to make friends or to keep friends?

Have you ever been disappointed or let down by a friend? If so, write about it below.

....

....

Did you know that God is a forever friend? He never grows tired of listening to you (Isaiah 65:24) and He is always willing to help (Isaiah 41:10). Unlike your other friends, His friendship is forever and won't fade or disappoint.

"The LORD was with Joseph, so he succeeded in everything he did as he served in the home of his Egyptian master."

Genesis 39:2 (NLT)

In Genesis 39 we read that the Lord was with Joseph even though he was out of place in Egypt. Even when Joseph had no family and no friends Joseph knew he could rely on God.

Doodle your friend below!

Finishing Off

God, today I am feeling... (Circle or color)

Happy

Blessed

Anxious

Sad

Angry

I feel this way because ....

....

Today I am thankful for ....

Today I am praying for ....

....

Go to page 69 and fill in your "Monthly Mood Tracker" chart.

WEEK TWO
A Fish Out of Water

Today is: (Color the day of the week)

S M T W T F S

DAY FOUR

HARVESTING THE FRUIT

This week we have learned that we are children of God and that He calls us friends. Today we will learn another amazing truth about where we belong.

Read:

"But we are citizens of heaven, where the Lord Jesus Christ lives. And we are eagerly waiting for him to return as our Savior."
Philippians 3:20 (NLT)

Do you know what the word "citizen" means? It describes someone who belongs to a certain country. If you live in the United States, you are an American citizen. If you live in Canada, you are a Canadian citizen. The word citizen can be used to describe where we live or what country we belong to.

A passport is a book of information about you that proves which country you belong to. If you have ever flown outside of your country your parents probably gave you a passport to hold. A passport proves your citizenship.

Have you ever flown anywhere really amazing? Where did you go?

....

Read:

"In him you also, when you heard the word of truth, the gospel of your salvation, and believed in him, were sealed with the promised Holy Spirit."
Ephesians 1:13 (ESV)

Since a passport is an extremely valuable piece of information it would have been received it in a sealed envelope.

Did you know that God also "seals" His children with the Holy Spirit as proof that they are His? You won't be able to see the seal, it is invisible, but God sees it and it is how He knows that you belong to Him.

When I feel like I don't belong I can remember that ....

....

When I feel like God doesn't see me I can remember that ....

....

34

Use this space to journal. You can write about what you learned today,
your worries, your thoughts, or your prayers.

....

....

....

....

....

....

....

....

....

....

Finishing Off

God, today I am feeling... (Circle or color)

| Happy | Blessed | Anxious | Sad | Angry |

I feel this way because ....

....

Today I am thankful for ....

Today I am praying for ....

....

Go to page 69 and fill in your "Monthly Mood Tracker" chart.

Today is: (Color the day of the week)

S M T W T F S

DAY FIVE

REVIEW AND DISCUSS

Have you ever felt like you didn't belong anywhere? Write about your experience below.

....

....

....

....

This week you learned that you are God's very special treasure. He chose **you** to be a part of His family! How has learning this truth changed how you see yourself? Do you know just how loved you are by your Heavenly Father?

....

....

....

....

....

Go back through days 1-4 and look at what you have been praying for. How have you seen God answer your prayers this week?

....

....

....

Scripture Writing Challenge

Rewrite:
"See how very much our Father loves us, for he calls us his children, and that is what we are!"
1 John 3:1 (NLT)

....

....

....

....

Finishing Off

God, today I am feeling... (Circle or color)

Happy   **Blessed**   **Anxious**   **Sad**   **Angry**

I feel this way because ....

....

Today I am thankful for ....

Today I am praying for ....

....

Go to page 69 and fill in your "Monthly Mood Tracker" chart.

Discussion Questions

• Week Two •

Pick one or more questions to discuss with your parents.

Kids ask your parents:

- Have you ever felt like you didn't belong?
- Have you ever felt like you didn't have any friends?
- Have you ever been let down by a friend?
- What did you learn through that time?

Parents ask your kids:

- Have you ever felt like you didn't belong?
- Are you having a hard time finding friends or keeping friends?
- What do you think is the difference between earthly friendships and God's friendship?
- How can I pray for you this week?

Family Prayer Requests:

....

....

....

....

Doodles

Use this empty space to draw or doodle!

Week Three
MARVELOUS MASTERPIECE
(Why did God create me?)

S M T W T F S

DAY ONE

PLANTING A SEED

Marvelous Masterpiece
(Why did God create me?)

"You made all the delicate, inner parts of my body and knit me together in my mother's womb. Thank you for making me so wonderfully complex! Your workmanship is marvelous, how well I know it."
Psalm 139:13-14 (NLT)

The Louvre Museum in Paris, France holds a number of famous and expensive pieces of artwork. You may have heard of the most famous of all—the Mona Lisa. Painted by Leonardo da Vinci in the year 1503, the Mona Lisa is the most famous work of art in all of history. It is valued at more than $500 million dollars.

That is an insane amount of money. In fact, it can be hard for us to understand exactly how big of a number 500 million is. Is it possible to count that high?

Determined to find out just exactly how long it would take someone to count to just 1 million, a man named Jeremy Harper recorded himself counting up to 1 million out loud. Only taking breaks to sleep, eat, and use the bathroom, Mr. Harper recited numbers out loud from a computer monitor on average 16 hours a day. When Mr. Harper finally reached 1 million he recorded 89 straight days counting.

Now consider the fact that the Mona Lisa is 500 times more than 1 million. In other words, it would take Mr. Harper approximately 122 years to count to 500 million! Leonardo da Vinci's Mona Lisa is an incredible masterpiece which is what makes it so valuable. However, even with a price tag of over half a billion dollars it's value still has a limit.

Now consider this... Did you know that you are God's incredible masterpiece? The worth and value He places on you is far greater than any piece of artwork in a gallery. 1 Corinthians 6:20 says, "For you were bought with a price..." The price being the precious blood of God's only son, Jesus Christ.

The Bible says that before you were born God had already thought very carefully about how He wanted to make you. Just as an artist staring at a blank canvas will carefully consider what colors to use or what tools would work best for his/her masterpiece, there was not one detail about you that God did not consider. Similar to how no two paintings have the same colors or brush strokes, so no two human beings are exactly the same either. Even identical twins are not perfectly the same.

God is the ultimate artist because unlike any other form of art our Creator does not make mistakes. Since God is the ultimate Creator and you are His creation, you are priceless. Unlike the Mona Lisa, there is no dollar amount that can ever compare to how valuable you are to God.

42

Use this space to journal. You can write about what you learned today, your worries, your thoughts, or your prayers.

....

....

....

....

....

....

....

....

Finishing Off

God, today I am feeling... (Circle or color)

Happy   **Blessed**   **Anxious**   **Sad**   **Angry**

I feel this way because ....

....

Today I am thankful for ....

Today I am praying for ....

....

Go to page 69 and fill in your "Monthly Mood Tracker" chart.

Today is: (Color the day of the week)

S M T W T F S

DAY TWO
WATERING FOR GROWTH

Yesterday we learned about how God created us as one-of-a-kind people. We also learned that we are priceless in His eyes. Today, we are going to learn in more detail how God designed the first humans on Earth, Adam and Eve.

Read:

"So God created human beings in his own image. In the image of God he created them; male and female he created them."

Genesis 1:27 (NLT)

When God created human beings He made two different genders, what were they? (Write them below)

.... **and** ....

How did God create you? Did He make you a boy or a girl? (Circle or color)

MALE (BOY)

FEMALE (GIRL)

Read:

"Then God looked over all he had made, and he saw that it was very good!"

Genesis 1:31 (NLT)

Look at the verse above and then fill in the blank.

"God looked over all he had made, and saw that it was .... *"*

Male and female. The Bible shows us that God made Adam and Eve different from each other and there was no one else exactly like either of them. Not only that, He called His design of male and female very good. Tomorrow we will learn about what this means for you and me.

44

I am the only girl in a family of 3 brothers, can you believe that? The boys are always having more fun than me. They get to share a bedroom with bunk beds and they are always spending time together because they like the same things. Sometimes I look at some of my friends who are girls and I feel like I am so different. I don't care about dressing pretty or about boys. Sometimes **I feel left out** and I wish that God made me a boy instead.

God made you exactly how He wanted you. He does not make mistakes!
What is something you love about being a boy or a girl?

....

....

....

Finishing Off

God, today I am feeling... (Circle or color)

Happy

Blessed

Anxious

Sad

Angry

I feel this way because ....

....

Today I am thankful for ....

Today I am praying for ....

....

Go to page 69 and fill in your "Monthly Mood Tracker" chart.

Today is: (Color the day of the week)

S   M   T   W   T   F   S

DAY THREE

GROWING ROOTS

Yesterday we learned that God created male
and female different from one another and
that He called His creation, "very good!"
Today we will look at how that truth applies to you.

Read again:
"Then God looked over all he had made, and he saw that it was very good!"
Genesis 1:31 (NLT)

If God called His creation of Adam and Eve "very good", how do you think He feels about
your body and how He has made you? Fill in the blank.

He thinks my body is ....

Read:
**"I praise you because I am fearfully and wonderfully made; your works are wonderful,
I know that full well."**
Psalm 139:14 (NIV)

Is there something about your appearance that you are self-conscious about?
Write it below.

....

How does God want us to respond to how He has made us? Look again at Psalm 139:14
and fill in the blank.

"I .... **you because I am fearfully and wonderfully made."**

Did you catch it? God wants us to PRAISE Him for how He made us because we are
fearfully and wonderfully made! The word fearfully means to be distinct, separated, set
apart. It means that when God created you He made you different from everyone else. He
not only decided before you were born if you were going to be a boy or girl but he also
decided every detail about your body including your hair color, height, eye color, nose
shape, body shape, etc.

If God calls His creation very good, how can that truth change the way you feel about your
body or how you look?

46

You are God's masterpiece! In the frame below, draw a picture of yourself.

Finishing Off

God, today I am feeling... (Circle or color)

Happy

Blessed

Anxious

Sad

Angry

I feel this way because ....

....

Today I am thankful for ....

Today I am praying for ....

....

47

Go to page 69 and fill in your "Monthly Mood Tracker" chart.

WEEK THREE
Marvelous Masterpiece

DAY FOUR
HARVESTING THE FRUIT

If God created us and decided every detail of how we would look are looks all that matters to Him? Today we will learn about what matters most to God.

Have you ever had someone say something really nice about your looks? How did you feel? Write about it below.

....

....

Have you ever been teased about what you look like? How did you feel? Write about it below.

....

....

Our bodies are a work of art, a masterpiece of God Himself. However, our looks should never determine how we feel about ourselves. Sometimes we can let hurtful comments or even compliments trick us into believing that our value lies solely in what we look like.

When God created you He also created your heart as well as your outward appearance. Our bodies are just a temporary home for our spirits which will one day live in Heaven with Jesus (2 Corinthians 5:1). But the heart is the very soul of a person. Our hearts are our very personalities, interests, passions, and emotions. The heart is what drives everything we do. It is also the most important thing to God.

Read:

"The Lord does not look at the things people look at. People look at the outward appearance, but the Lord looks at the heart."

1 Samuel 16:7b (NIV)

It can be easy to be focused on what we look like but the Bible tells us that God is far more interested in the appearance of our hearts. People will look at us and see the outward appearance but God is more focused on our hearts.

Have you been placing too much value in your outward appearance? How can you shift your focus off your appearance and onto your heart? Journal your thoughts.

....

....

On the next page, look up Galatians 5:22-23 to learn about what kind of heart qualities are important to God.

48

Look up Galatians 5:22-23 and write each fruit of the spirit.

FRUITS
of the
SPIRIT
Gal. 5:22-23

Finishing Off

God, today I am feeling... (Circle or color)

Happy

Blessed

Anxious

Sad

Angry

I feel this way because ....

....

Today I am thankful for ....

Today I am praying for ....

....

49

Go to page 69 and fill in your "Monthly Mood Tracker" chart.

WEEK THREE
Marvelous Masterpiece

Today is: (Color the day of the week)

(S) (M) (T) (W) (T) (F) (S)

DAY FIVE

REVIEW AND DISCUSS

This week we learned that we are fearfully and wonderfully made and that God does not make mistakes. Have you ever struggled to believe this truth? If so, write about it below. If not, write a prayer thanking God for how He has made you.

....

....

....

....

....

According to what you learned, are people's outward appearances important? How can what you learned start to change how you see yourself and/or others around you?

....

....

....

How have you seen God answer your prayers this week?

....

....

....

Scripture Writing Challenge

Rewrite:
"I praise you because I am fearfully and wonderfully made; your works are wonderful,
I know that full well."

Psalm 139:14 (NIV)

....

....

....

....

Finishing Off

God, today I am feeling... (Circle or color)

Happy

Blessed

Anxious

Sad

Angry

I feel this way because ....
....

Today I am thankful for ....

Today I am praying for ....

....

Go to page 69 and fill in your "Monthly Mood Tracker" chart.

Discussion Questions

• Week Three •

Pick one or more questions to discuss with your parents.

Kids ask your parents:

- Have you ever felt unhappy about your body?
- Do you think God makes mistakes when He creates people?
- What is one physical feature about me that you love?

Parents ask your kids:

- Have you ever felt unhappy about your body?
- What did you learn this week about how God has made you?
- Have you ever been teased about how you look? Why do you think God cares about our hearts far more than our appearance?
- How can I pray for you this week?

Family Prayer Requests:

....

....

....

....

Doodles

Use this empty space to draw or doodle!

Week Four
GIFTS FROM HEAVEN
(Why did God give me gifts and abilities?)

Today is: (Color the day of the week)

(S) (M) (T) (W) (T) (F) (S)

DAY ONE

PLANTING A SEED

Gifts From Heaven
(Why did God give me gifts and abilities?)

*"God has given each of you a gift from his great variety
of spiritual gifts. Use them well to serve one another."*
1 Peter 4:10 (NLT)

"'Twas the night before Christmas and all through the house, not a creature was stirring, not even a mouse." Are you familiar with this famous Christmas poem? If we were to be honest most kids would say that Christmas Eve was anything but calm. In fact, most kids would probably admit that they usually spend the night before Christmas awake in their beds counting the hours before they can jump out of bed, run downstairs, and open their gifts! Can you relate? What is your favorite gift you have ever been given?

You may not be aware of the fact that your parents will often spend a lot of time considering which gifts they want to give you on Christmas Day. Your parents will want to give you something you will really enjoy. They will also try to pick something that they know you will get a lot of use out of. Something that after time won't sit on the shelf collecting dust.

James 1:17 says that, "Every good and perfect gift is from above, coming down from the Father of the heavenly lights." Similar to the presents you are given at Christmas, the Bible says that God has also given each of us gifts and abilities.

Maybe you are an amazing artist, an athlete, or can sing a song on key with very little effort. Maybe you are great at organizing, can crunch numbers like a whiz, or can build things with your hands that inspire people. Do you have a gift of helping others? Encouraging people? Making people laugh? Whatever gift He has given you, He has given it to you for a special reason. His desire is that we use our gifts to the fullest of our ability to honor Him.

What kinds of gifts do you think God may have given you? What sorts of things do you naturally excel at?

It is exciting to think that like a gift sitting under the Christmas tree waiting to be opened, God has also given you certain gifts and abilities that He is excited to see you use! This week we will learn how to identify the gifts God has given you, how to use those gifts in a way that will help others, and make the giver (God) happy.

56

Use this space to journal. You can write about what you learned today, your worries, your thoughts, or your prayers.

....

....

....

....

....

....

....

....

....

Finishing Off

God, today I am feeling... (Circle or color)

Happy   **Blessed**   **Anxious**   **Sad**   **Angry**

I feel this way because ....

....

Today I am thankful for ....

Today I am praying for ....

....

Go to page 69 and fill in your "Monthly Mood Tracker" chart.

Today is: (Color the day of the week)

(S) (M) (T) (W) (T) (F) (S)

DAY TWO

WATERING FOR GROWTH

Yesterday we learned that God
is the giver of every good and perfect gift
(James 1:17). You have been given gifts and abilities.
Do you know what they might be? Fill in the blank below.

I think I am gifted at ....

Now that you have an idea of what your gifting might be, the question is "Now what?"

When Jesus was on Earth, He often taught people by using stories called parables.
In Matthew 25:14-30, we read about a parable that Jesus told about a master and his 3
servants. The master decided to go on a long trip so he gave each servant an amount of
money (called "talents") and trusted that they would be wise with what they were given.
The first two servants invested their money wisely but the third was not so wise.

Read:
"But the servant who received the one bag of silver dug a hole in the ground and hid the master's money."
Matthew 25:18 (NLT)

Can you believe it? The third servant buried the "talent" he was given. Can you imagine
receiving a gift at Christmas then burying it in your backyard?
What a shame that would be!

God might not have given you money but the Bible is clear that He has given each of us
certain gifts and abilities. Just like the servants in Jesus' story—God wants us using what
He has given us well.

What about you? Look above at where you wrote down what you think you might be
gifted at.

Read:
"Do not neglect your gift, which was given you through prophecy when the body of elders laid their hands on you."
1 Timothy 4:14 (NIV)

Are you using your gifting well?

 Yes No

How often are you using the gift that God gave you? Are you working at
growing in that skill or are you "burying" your gifts?

58

Is there a gift you have that you are too shy to use? Write about it below.

....

....

....

Finishing Off

God, today I am feeling... (Circle or color)

Happy

Blessed

Anxious

Sad

Angry

I feel this way because ....

....

Today I am thankful for ....

Today I am praying for ....

....

Go to page 69 and fill in your "Monthly Mood Tracker" chart.

WEEK FOUR
Gifts from Heaven

Today is: (Color the day of the week)

S M T W T F S

DAY THREE

GROWING ROOTS

We know that all of us have been given gifts and abilities and that God wants us to use our gifts wisely. Did you know that using our gifts wisely goes beyond using them for our own enjoyment? God has bigger purposes for the gifts He gave you.

Read:

"God has given each of you a gift from his great variety of spiritual gifts. Use them well to serve one another."

1 Peter 4:10 (NLT)

In the verse above we read that God has given us all gifts. He also tells us how He wants us to use our gifts. Look at the last sentence in 1 Peter 4:10 and fill in the blank.

"Use them well to .... *one another."*

There are so many ways we can use our gifts to serve someone.

If you are good at math, you can help other kids with their homework. If you are good at baking, you can bake cookies for someone to brighten their day. If you are artistic, you can paint or draw a picture to bless someone. If you are good at encouraging people, you can give a friend a boost of confidence by pointing out something they are really good at.

Yesterday you wrote down something you are good at. Write it again below.

....

How can you begin to use your gift today to serve someone? Journal some ideas below.

....

....

....

Use the space below to doodle something that represents your special gift or ability!

Finishing Off

God, today I am feeling... (Circle or color)

Happy   Blessed   Anxious   Sad   Angry

I feel this way because ....

....

Today I am thankful for ....

Today I am praying for ....

....

Go to page 69 and fill in your "Monthly Mood Tracker" chart.

WEEK FOUR
Gifts from Heaven

DAY FOUR

HARVESTING THE FRUIT

This week we have learned that God has given each of us gifts. He wants us to use our gifts wisely and to serve each other.

But have you ever looked at someone else's gifts and felt jealous? Maybe you wish that God gave you a different one instead. Someone else's gifts might even seem more important than yours.

Read:

"The human body has many parts, but the many parts make up one whole body. So it is with the body of Christ."

1 Corinthians 12:12 (NLT)

Here's a challenge for you: try drinking a cup of water with your feet, or how about playing a game of dodgeball blindfolded, try singing a song with your mouth closed, or jumping rope on your knees. Do these challenges sound difficult? Even impossible?

In 1 Corinthians 12:12 we read that each person in God's family is like a body part. No part is unimportant or less significant than the next. Have you ever broken your arm or your leg? Suddenly, every day things become very difficult. You probably never realized how important your arm or leg was until it was broken. It is the same with your gift. Although it may seem insignificant, God has gifted you and that gift is a big deal!

In the space below, write out a prayer to God thanking Him for the gift(s) He has given you. Ask for Him to show you how you can use your gifts to serve others.

Dear God, ...

....

....

....

....

In Jesus' name, Amen.

Use this space to journal. You can write about what you learned today, your worries, your thoughts, or your prayers.

....

....

....

....

....

....

....

....

Finishing Off

God, today I am feeling... (Circle or color)

Happy   **Blessed**   **Anxious**   **Sad**   **Angry**

I feel this way because ....

....

Today I am thankful for ....

Today I am praying for ....

....

Go to page 69 and fill in your "Monthly Mood Tracker" chart.

WEEK FOUR
Gifts from Heaven

DAY FIVE
REVIEW AND DISCUSS

Why do you think it can be easy to "bury" your gifts? From what you learned this week, why does God want you to use the gifts He has given you?

....

....

....

....

....

Think about the people around you at school, home, church, or in your neighborhood. Chances are high that there is someone in your life that can benefit from your gifts.

Think of some people in your life who you can serve this week. Write one name below.

.... (Someone at school)

.... (Someone at home)

.... (Someone at my church)

.... (Someone in my neighborhood)

How have you seen God answer your prayers this week?

....

....

64

Scripture Writing Challenge

Rewrite:
"God has given each of you a gift from his great variety of spiritual gifts. Use them well to serve one another."

1 Peter 4:10 (NLT)

....

....

....

....

Finishing Off

God, today I am feeling... (Circle or color)

Happy

Blessed

Anxious

Sad

Angry

I feel this way because ....

....

Today I am thankful for ....

Today I am praying for ....

....

Go to page 69 and fill in your "Monthly Mood Tracker" chart.

Discussion Questions
• Week Four •

Pick one or more questions to discuss with your parents.

Kids ask your parents:

- What gifts or abilities do you think God gave you?
- Have you ever used those gifts to help someone?
- What gifts or abilities do you think I have?

Parents ask your kids:

- What gifts or abilities do you think you have?
- Were you able to use your gifts this week help someone?
- How can I pray for you this week?

Family Prayer Requests:

....

....

....

....

Doodles

Use this empty space to draw or doodle!

MONTHLY MOOD

TRACKER

CHAPTER ONE

Color a dot under how you are feeling today.

 Angry

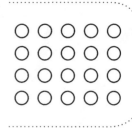
○ ○ ○ ○ ○
○ ○ ○ ○ ○
○ ○ ○ ○ ○
○ ○ ○ ○ ○

 Sad

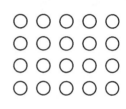
○ ○ ○ ○ ○
○ ○ ○ ○ ○
○ ○ ○ ○ ○
○ ○ ○ ○ ○

 Anxious

○ ○ ○ ○ ○
○ ○ ○ ○ ○
○ ○ ○ ○ ○
○ ○ ○ ○ ○

 Blessed

○ ○ ○ ○ ○
○ ○ ○ ○ ○
○ ○ ○ ○ ○
○ ○ ○ ○ ○

 Happy

○ ○ ○ ○ ○
○ ○ ○ ○ ○
○ ○ ○ ○ ○
○ ○ ○ ○ ○

CHAPTER 1 MOOD TRACKER CHART

Chapter Two
GOD HELPS

"Behold, God is my helper; the Lord is the sustainer of my soul!"

Psalm 54:4 (NASB)

Week One
LOOK TO THE HILLS
(Where can I go when I am afraid?)

WEEK ONE
Look to the Hills

Today is: (Color the day of the week)

S M T W T F S

Look to the Hills
(Where can I go when I am afraid?)

DAY ONE

PLANTING A SEED

> "And Elisha prayed, 'Open his eyes, LORD, so that he may see.'
> Then the LORD opened the servant's eyes, and he looked and saw
> the hills full of horses and chariots of fire all around Elisha."
>
> 2 Kings 6:17 (NIV)

Chances are high that you know someone who has glasses. Glasses are used to correct vision problems for people who have a hard time focusing. People who are near-sighted have no problem seeing things up close but seeing things in the distance is really difficult. The right set of lenses can correct the problem by putting things far away suddenly into focus again. Glasses are a great tool to help us clearly see the world around us.

In the book of 2 Kings, the Bible talks about the prophet Elisha (a man who speaks for God) and his servant, Gehazi. Elisha knew that the King of Aram was planning a surprise attack on the Israelites and warned the King of Israel. But when the King of Aram found out that his plan was ruined he sent horses and chariots to attack the Israelites under the cover of darkness.

The Israelites were surprised, outnumbered, and unprepared to fight. A quick glance at the army that surrounded them was enough to cause Gehazi to panic. How on earth could they defeat this army when the Armean army was far bigger than their own? It was an impossible situation. It's safe to say that Gehazi was freaking out!

But the prophet Elisha was filled with God's peace and instead of joining in the panic he prayed for God to help his servant see the situation clearly. Immediately, Gehazi's eyes were opened and he saw hills full of horses and chariots of fire all around them (2 Kings 6:17). God caused Gehazi to see the entire situation clearly. They weren't alone at all! God's heavenly army of angels surrounded Elisha and his servant and they were ready to fight for the Israelites.

Sometimes when we are facing something overwhelming we feel powerless. Our eyes may only see the problem in front of us and we can also suffer from a lack of near-sightedness too. We can feel alone and lose focus of God's power in our situation. Our troubles, fears, and anxieties in front of us can be so real we can forget what else surrounds us; God's power and help. Like Elisha and Gehazi, God's heavenly armies are on our side prepared to go to battle for us and help us conquer whatever fears or worries we may have.

This week we will learn how to keep our focus on God when we are afraid, anxious, or worried so that we can remain focused on God's power and help.

74

Use this space to journal. You can write about what you learned today, your worries, your thoughts, or your prayers.

....

....

....

....

....

....

....

....

Finishing Off

God, today I am feeling... (Circle or color)

Happy   **Blessed**   **Anxious**   **Sad**   **Angry**

I feel this way because ....

....

Today I am thankful for ....

Today I am praying for ....

....

Go to page 129 and fill in your "Monthly Mood Tracker" chart.

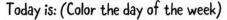
Today is: (Color the day of the week)

S M T W T F S

DAY TWO
WATERING FOR GROWTH

Yesterday we read about Elisha and Gehazi
and a big battle that they were facing. When Elisha
prayed for their spiritual vision they were able to see
a powerful army of God's angels on their side.

What kinds of things are kids usually afraid of? Can you list some common fears below?

....

Are you facing any fears or worries right now?
Our fears can range from tests, to something bad happening to us or our family, fears of
failure, the dark, insects, needles, or even a fear of death.

Sometimes I worry about ....

Have you talked to a parent about your fears?

 Yes   No

If not, what is stopping you?

Read:
"Don't worry about anything; instead, pray about everything. Tell God what you need, and thank
him for all he has done."
Philippians 4:6 (NLT)

Using a pencil or marker, underline what the Bible tells us to do instead of worrying.

In the space below, write out a prayer to God about your fears. Don't forget to ask Him to
help you focus on His power and help.

Dear God, I am worried or afraid of...

....

....

In Jesus' name, Amen.

76

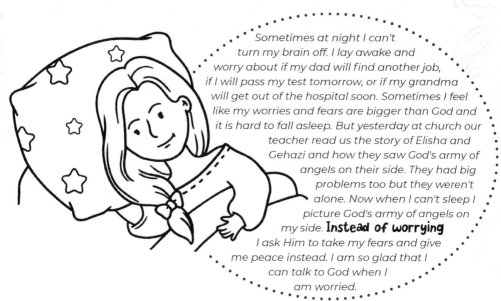

Sometimes at night I can't turn my brain off. I lay awake and worry about if my dad will find another job, if I will pass my test tomorrow, or if my grandma will get out of the hospital soon. Sometimes I feel like my worries and fears are bigger than God and it is hard to fall asleep. But yesterday at church our teacher read us the story of Elisha and Gehazi and how they saw God's army of angels on their side. They had big problems too but they weren't alone. Now when I can't sleep I picture God's army of angels on my side. **Instead of worrying** *I ask Him to take my fears and give me peace instead. I am so glad that I can talk to God when I am worried.*

Write about a time when your worries or fears kept you up at night. What did you do?

....

....

Finishing Off

God, today I am feeling... (Circle or color)

Happy   **Blessed**   **Anxious**   **Sad**   **Angry**

I feel this way because ....

....

Today I am thankful for ....

Today I am praying for ....

....

77

Go to page 129 and fill in your "Monthly Mood Tracker" chart.

Today is: (Color the day of the week)

S   M   T   W   T   F   S

Today we will learn about where we can
go when we are worried or afraid.

Read:

*"This I declare about the LORD: He alone is my refuge, my place of safety;
he is my God, and I trust him. For he will rescue you from every trap and protect you from
deadly disease. He will cover you with his feathers. He will shelter you with his wings. His
faithful promises are your armor and protection."*

Psalm 91:2-4 (NLT)

Have you ever experienced a severe storm? Depending on where you live the kinds
of storms you will see will vary from thunderstorms, to blizzards, tornadoes, or even
hurricanes. Have you ever been caught in a storm that was really scary?
What happened? Use the next page to journal about it.

Now have another look at the verse above. There is a word repeated in the verse
above. Circle the words **protect** and **protection**.

Think about what you are afraid of. Write it again below.

I am afraid or worried about ....

Look at Psalm 91:2-4 again. The Bible uses an example of a certain animal to help us
understand how God reacts when His children are afraid. What animal do you think
God is talking about in this verse? (Hint: feathers and wings are used to describe it!)

....

(Name of the animal)

If you guessed a bird, you are right! God uses a beautiful example in this verse by
comparing His love and protection over us to how a mother bird will gather her
chicks under her wings during a storm. Chicks are born with very little feathers so
God not only designed the feathers of their mother to be waterproof but to be a
warm, protective place for her chicks. When a storm hits her chicks know that the
safest place to be is under her wings.

Is there a storm of worry or fear in your heart right now? God promises that He is our
safe place and protection from anything and everything that worries us. Like a
mother bird who gathers her little ones and protects them when they are afraid so
God promises the same for us. There is no fear or worry that is too big for God!

Have you ever been caught in a bad storm that frightened you?
Describe how you felt and what you did.

....

....

....

....

....

....

....

....

....

Finishing Off

God, today I am feeling... (Circle or color)

Happy   Blessed   Anxious   Sad   Angry

I feel this way because ....

....

Today I am thankful for ....

Today I am praying for ....

....

Go to page 129 and fill in your "Monthly Mood Tracker" chart.

Today is: (Color the day of the week)

S M T W T F S

DAY FOUR

HARVESTING THE FRUIT

This week we learned how God helped Elisha and Gehazi fight a big battle with an army of angels. We also learned that fears and worries can sometimes feel like out of control storms for which we need God's protection.

Just like God sent mighty angels to fight for Elisha and the Israelites, God has also put angels in your life to protect you too.

Read:

"For he will order his angels to protect you wherever you go."
Psalm 91:11 (NLT)

Are you beginning to see just how BIG our God is compared to your fears and worries?

Like Gehazi, we can become so focused on our fears that we can forget that God's power is on our side and that we are not alone. Picture fear as fuzzy mold which thrives in the dark. Left in the dark our fears can grow and become bigger problems too.

On the next page is a fear jar. Inside the jar draw a picture of something that represents your fear or worry.

Now imagine God taking the jar, sealing it tight, and lovingly taking it from your hands. He wants you to bring your fears and anxieties to Him. Have you done that yet or are you facing your fear alone?

Read:

"See, God has come to save me. I will trust in him and not be afraid. The Lord God is my strength and my song; he has given me victory."
Isaiah 12:2 (NLT)

Circle the word **victory**.
Just like God gave Elisha and Gehazi victory in their battle, God wants to give you victory over your fears and worries too. If you don't know where to start prayer is always a good choice.

Dear God, thank you that you promise me safety. Thank you that you protect me and that I do not need to be afraid. God I ask you for victory over my fears. Help me to see your powerful help and fill me with your peace.

In Jesus' name, Amen.

80

Inside the jar, doodle or write some things you are afraid of or worry about.

Finishing Off

God, today I am feeling... (Circle or color)

Happy

Blessed

Anxious

Sad

Angry

I feel this way because ....
....

Today I am thankful for ....

Today I am praying for ....
....

81

Go to page 129 and fill in your "Monthly Mood Tracker" chart.

WEEK ONE
Look to the Hills

Today is: (Color the day of the week)

S M T W T F S

DAY FIVE

REVIEW AND DISCUSS

According to what we learned this week, how can you keep your focus on God when you are afraid, anxious, or worried? (Go back and read page 74 if you aren't sure.)

....

....

....

....

....

Think about a fear you have been focusing on this week. How has what you learned this week helped you? Do you believe that God can help you conquer that fear?

....

....

....

....

....

How have you seen God answer your prayers this week?

....

....

Scripture Writing Challenge

Rewrite:

"See, God has come to save me. I will trust in him and not be afraid. The Lord God is my strength and my song; he has given me victory."

Isaiah 12:2 (NLT)

....

....

....

....

Finishing Off

God, today I am feeling... (Circle or color)

Happy

Blessed

Anxious

Sad

Angry

I feel this way because ....

....

Today I am thankful for ....

Today I am praying for ....

....

Go to page 129 and fill in your "Monthly Mood Tracker" chart.

Discussion Questions
• Week One •

Pick one or more questions to discuss with your parents.

Kids ask your parents:

- What were you afraid of when you were my age?
- Do you ever feel afraid or worried as an adult?
- What do you do when you feel afraid?

Parents ask your kids:

- What did you draw in your fear jar on page 81?
- What do you think God wants to give you instead of fear?
- What have you learned about God this week?
- How can I pray for you this week?

Family Prayer Requests:

....

....

....

....

Doodles

Use this empty space to draw or doodle!

Week Two
WEAK AT BEST
(Can God use even me?)

Today is: (Color the day of the week)

S M T W T F S

DAY ONE

PLANTING A SEED

Weak At Best
(Can God use even me?)

"They said to all the people of Israel, 'The land we traveled through and explored is a wonderful land! And if the Lord is pleased with us, he will bring us safely into that land and give it to us. It is a rich land flowing with milk and honey. Do not rebel against the Lord, and don't be afraid of the people of the land. They are only helpless prey to us! They have no protection, but the Lord is with us! Don't be afraid of them!'"

Numbers 14:7-9 (NLT)

It is 40 years after Moses has answered the call to lead the Israelites out of Pharaoh's back-breaking labor and harsh leadership to a land of freedom. The Israelites had come to the edge of the land God promised them, the land of Canaan. Forty years of wandering the desert and hard lessons were about to pay off.

But when Moses sent out spies to look at Canaan they saw strong cities with strong men and they were terrified (Numbers 13:28). They knew that God's rich blessing was in Canaan and that God had already promised them victory but the fear of the unknown kept the Israelites back from receiving God's wonderful blessings.

God must have been heartbroken. If only the Israelites could step out and trust that He had their backs what wonderful things awaited them. God knew they weren't perfect, 40 years of watching the Israelites wander proved it. But God still had plans for them despite their imperfections, He knew they were afraid. He wanted His children to trust Him and to obey regardless of how they felt.

Like Moses and the Israelites refusing to act it can be easy to let the fear of failure or fear of the unknown keep us from trying something hard. Sometimes God will call us out of our comfort zones because He has wonderful blessings in store for us when we obey.

Maybe He is asking you to use the gifts and abilities He gave you to serve Him but you are too shy. Perhaps He is asking you to invite a friend to church or maybe He is asking you to try something new but you don't feel smart enough, brave enough, or strong enough. Maybe you are seeing something happening around you that you know is wrong and you know God wants you to speak up but you are afraid of what will happen.

Like the Israelites hiding in their comfortable tents, God will often times call us out of our comfort zones too. God never expects us to do everything perfectly because He knows that we are weak. But God promises that His help and grace is all we need. He has big plans for us!

88

Use this space to journal. You can write about what you learned today, your worries, your thoughts, or your prayers.

COMFORT ZONE

GROWTH

CONVENIENT

FAITH

....
....
....
....
....
....
....
....
....
....

Finishing Off

God, today I am feeling... (Circle or color)

Happy   Blessed   Anxious   Sad   Angry

I feel this way because ....

....

Today I am thankful for ....

Today I am praying for ....

....

89

Go to page 129 and fill in your "Monthly Mood Tracker" chart.

WEEK TWO
Weak at Best

DAY TWO
WATERING FOR GROWTH

Moses called God for a big job—leading hundreds of thousands of Israelites out of Egypt into the Promised Land of Canaan. Even though God promised to be with him, Moses still struggled with feeling not good enough.

Read:

" 'Now go, for I am sending you to Pharaoh. You must lead my people Israel out of Egypt.' But Moses protested to God, 'Who am I to appear before Pharaoh? Who am I to lead the people of Israel out of Egypt?' "

Exodus 3:10-11 (NLT)

Circle the word **protested**.

To protest means to strongly disagree with something. You probably do this at home without realizing it. Have you ever protested against doing chores? Or maybe you are a pro at protesting when it's time to do your homework. We can protest God's call in all kinds of different ways too. Think about a time when you knew God was asking you to do the right thing but you did not do it. Maybe your protest was, "I can't do that! I'll look silly!" or, "If I say something everyone will think I am a goody-goody," or "There is no way I am doing that, I am not even good at that!"

After God gave Moses his instructions, Moses immediately protested to God. "Who am I to appear before Pharaoh? Who am I to lead the people of Israel out of Egypt?" Moses did not feel like he was the best person for the job for a reason.

Read:

"But Moses pleaded with the Lord, 'O Lord, I'm not very good with words. I never have been, and I'm not now, even though you have spoken to me. I get tongue-tied, and my words get tangled.' "

Exodus 4:10 (NLT)

Look at the verses above. Moses had a weakness, what was it?

Moses wasn't very good at ....

Was Moses perfect?   **Yes**   **No**

God wasn't interested in Moses' shortcomings. He simply wanted Moses to trust and obey despite his imperfections. Moses did not have to worry because God already had plans to help. God sends Aaron with Moses who helps him speak to Pharaoh.

What does that mean for you and me? Does God expect perfection from us when He asks us to do something? Does God expect perfection from you?

90

Our church youth group has been asked to volunteer at a nursing home next weekend. I guess a lot of people in nursing homes do not have visitors very often and our youth pastor told us that a lot of the seniors were really lonely. He seemed to think that a visit from our youth group would be really encouraging for the residents at the home. A lot of the kids are excited, some of them have made cards or even baked cookies to give to the residents but I am nervous. **I don't know how** to talk to strangers and I worry that I will say the wrong thing. I know God wants to use me to encourage someone but I don't know how.

Write about a time when you had to do something outside of your comfort zone.

....

....

....

Finishing Off

God, today I am feeling... (Circle or color)

Happy   Blessed   Anxious   Sad   Angry

I feel this way because ....

....

Today I am thankful for ....

Today I am praying for ....

....

Go to page 129 and fill in your "Monthly Mood Tracker" chart.

WEEK TWO
Weak at Best

Today is: (Color the day of the week)

S M T W T F S

DAY THREE

GROWING ROOTS

God had big plans for Moses! Even though Moses protested at first God gave Moses exactly what He needed to accomplish His plan for him.

Did you know that God has big plans for you too and that He also will provide you with exactly what you need to do His will?

Read:

"For we are God's masterpiece. He has created us anew in Christ Jesus, so we can do the good things he planned for us long ago."
Ephesians 2:10 (NLT)

Circle the phrase *good things he planned for us long ago*.

In Chapter 1, week 3, we learned that God creates us as masterpieces and that He knew us before we were even born. We also learned that God gave us gifts and abilities for a purpose. God's plans for us began even before the world was created! He knew exactly what He wanted us to do and He also gave us everything we need to accomplish His plans for us.

Read:

"may he equip you with all you need for doing his will. May he produce in you, through the power of Jesus Christ, every good thing that is pleasing to him. All glory to him forever and ever! Amen."
Hebrews 13:21 (NLT)

Circle the word **equip**.
The word equip means to be given everything that is needed to accomplish a task.

Think about this... would your parents ask you to brush your teeth without providing you with a toothbrush or toothpaste? Would they ask you to make your bed without providing you with bedding? Would they ask you to take a shower without giving you soap and shampoo? Or ask you to eat your dinner without giving you the utensils you need?

Just like God provided Moses with Aaron, God never asks us to do something without giving us exactly what we need to do it. God helps us by providing the gifts, abilities, courage, or even other people to help us.

God has big plans for you! Whatever it is He has asked you to do He will also give you exactly what you need to obey Him.

92

God has big plans for you! Doodle a picture of what you think that may look like. What do you want to be when you get older?

Finishing Off

God, today I am feeling... (Circle or color)

Happy   Blessed   Anxious   Sad   Angry

I feel this way because ....

....

Today I am thankful for ....

Today I am praying for ....

....

93

Go to page 129 and fill in your "Monthly Mood Tracker" chart.

WEEK TWO
Weak at Best

Today is: (Color the day of the week)

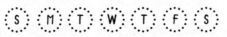

(S) (M) (T) (W) (T) (F) (S)

DAY FOUR

HARVESTING THE FRUIT

This week we learned that God asked Moses to do a big job which Moses felt totally unprepared for. Moses had a weakness; he had a hard time speaking clearly but God wasn't interested in Moses' strengths or weaknesses. He just wanted Moses to obey.

Sometimes God will call us to step out of our comfort zones into something new. God's call might not always be something that we are good at but that is OK! We do not have to worry about doing everything perfectly.

Read:

"Each time he said, 'My grace is all you need. My power works best in weakness.' So now I am glad to boast about my weaknesses, so that the power of Christ can work through me."
2 Corinthians 12:9 (NLT)

Most people find it easier to boast about what they are good at but God tells us to do the opposite. 2 Corinthians 12:9 says that God's power works best when we admit we are weak and that we need Him. Moses wasn't a good speaker and God knew it. God already had plans to help Moses speak to Pharaoh.

Read:

" 'Don't be afraid', he said, 'for you are very precious to God. Peace! Be encouraged! Be strong!' As he spoke these words to me, I suddenly felt stronger and said to him, 'Please speak to me, my lord, for you have strengthened me. ' "
Daniel 10:19 (NLT)

Circle the phrase **Don't be afraid** and **Be encouraged! Be strong!**

God has big plans for you! Do you know what He is asking you to do? Is He asking you to try something new? To stand up for what is right? Is He asking you to invite someone to church or befriend someone who doesn't have friends? Is He asking you to help someone or use your gifts to please Him? Is He asking you to talk to an adult about something important?

I think God wants me to ....

I am afraid because ....

Daniel 10:19 tells us to not be afraid but to be encouraged and strong!
We are precious to Him and if we ask Him for His strength He will give it.
Is there something He is calling you to do? How can you step outside of your comfort zone and obey Him today?

94

Use this space to journal. You can write about what you learned today, your worries, your thoughts, or your prayers.

....

....

....

....

....

....

....

....

....

Finishing Off

God, today I am feeling... (Circle or color)

Happy   Blessed   Anxious   Sad   Angry

I feel this way because ....

....

Today I am thankful for ....

Today I am praying for ....

....

Go to page 129 and fill in your "Monthly Mood Tracker" chart.

WEEK TWO
Weak at Best

Talk to God about what you learned this week. What did you learn that was new? How can the story of Moses and his weakness with speaking encourage you today? Is God limited by our weaknesses?

....

....

....

....

....

Is there something you believe God is asking you to do but you are afraid? How do you plan to obey Him this week? How are you feeling about it?

....

....

....

....

....

How have you seen God answer your prayers this week?

....

....

96

Scripture Writing Challenge

Rewrite:

"Each time he said, 'My grace is all you need. My power works best in weakness.' So now I am glad to boast about my weaknesses, so that the power of Christ can work through me."

2 Corinthians 12:9 (NLT)

....

....

....

....

Finishing Off

God, today I am feeling... (Circle or color)

Happy   **Blessed**   **Anxious**   **Sad**   **Angry**

I feel this way because ....

....

Today I am thankful for ....

Today I am praying for ....

....

Go to page 129 and fill in your "Monthly Mood Tracker" chart.

Discussion Questions
• Week Two •

Pick one or more questions to discuss with your parents.

Kids ask your parents:

- Describe a time when God asked you to do something out of your comfort zone.
- Do you ever feel discouraged when you can't do things perfectly?
- Is there something in my life you think God is asking me to obey Him in?

Parents ask your kids:

- What did you learn this week about Moses? What was God asking him to do and what was Moses' response to God?
- Do you think God expects perfection from you? Why or why not?
- How can I pray for you this week?

Family Prayer Requests:

....

....

....

....

Doodles

Use this empty space to draw or doodle!

Week Three
STICK WITH IT
(I can do hard things!)

WEEK THREE
Stick With It

Today is: (Color the day of the week)

S M T W T F S

DAY ONE

PLANTING A SEED

Stick With It
(I can do hard things!)

"For you have need of endurance, so that when you have done the will of God you may receive what is promised."
Hebrews 10:36 (ESV)

At the playground you stare up at the monkey bars and jump to the first bar determined to finally make it all the way across. But halfway through you feel your hands slipping again and you fall to the ground frustrated.

You are at school trying to focus on the math problem on the white board and you feel yourself getting upset. It feels like no matter how hard you try you are never going to get it. You try your best to be a good friend but you accidentally say something hurtful and now your friend is angry with you. Have you ever felt like giving up on something?

Noah probably felt the same way. God told him to build a huge boat—something that had never been done before. This boat was to be 510 feet long—the size equal to one and a half football fields. Noah was not given a team to help him, the task of building the ark was entirely Noah's job. That's a really big job from God!

In fact, building the ark took Noah anywhere from 55-75 years to complete. Can you imagine 55-75 years doing the same job? It is likely that Noah made mistakes but he kept on building. Noah probably had times when he felt frustrated at the project God had given him, maybe he felt like giving up. He probably had to constantly ask for God's help. Noah needed a lot of perseverance!

When something feels difficult it is normal to feel overwhelmed and frustrated. We may want to give up or develop a habit of not finishing things when they feel hard. While it can be easy to get angry and give up it is really important to God that we learn how to persevere and see tasks through to the end.

At the end of the 75 years, the first drop of rain fell and Noah's hard work and perseverance paid off. Dry in the ark with his family and the animals, Noah enjoyed the safety and protection the ark brought. Noah enjoyed the blessing of sticking with his task.

This week we will learn about how God helps us stick with things when we want to give up and why perseverance is so important.

102

Use this space to journal. You can write about what you learned today,
your worries, your thoughts, or your prayers.

....

....

....

....

....

....

....

....

Finishing Off

God, today I am feeling... (Circle or color)

Happy   **Blessed**   **Anxious**   **Sad**   **Angry**

I feel this way because ....

....

Today I am thankful for ....

Today I am praying for ....

....

Go to page 129 and fill in your "Monthly Mood Tracker" chart.

Today is: (Color the day of the week)

(S) (M) (T) (W) (T) (F) (S)

DAY TWO

WATERING FOR GROWTH

What do Thomas Edison and former President Abraham Lincoln have in common? Surprisingly, both of these men knew what it was like to repeatedly fail. Thomas Edison failed 10,000 times before he finally perfected the incandescent light bulb. That is a lot of failure for one person! Abraham Lincoln lost 5 elections before finally becoming President of the United States in 1861. To persevere means to try something again and again, even when you fail.

Have you ever had something really difficult to do and you repeatedly failed? What was it and how did you feel? Write about it below.

....

....

Read:

"So let's not get tired of doing what is good. At just the right time we will reap a harvest of blessing if we don't give up."
Galatians 6:9 (NLT)

Circle the phrase **not get tired**.
Is there something you are working on that is really hard? Are you getting tired?

Look at Galatians 6:9 again. What are we promised if we don't give up? Fill in the blank.

"So let's not get tired of doing what is good. At just the right time we will reap a harvest of .... if we don't give up."

To "reap a harvest of blessing" means to enjoy the rewards of our hard work. When we stick to something that is hard and succeed we will enjoy the blessing that comes because we did not give up.

How about you? Is there a task or skill that you are trying to master but are frustrated with? Maybe it's a social skill you struggle with or a subject in school you find really hard. Is there a relationship in your life that is very difficult and you are tempted to give up?

Proverbs 16:3 tells us that if we commit our work to the Lord that we will succeed, especially if we are asking Him to help us make Him happy. God's help is always available to us when we need more perseverance.

104

Today in math my mom and I worked on trying to memorize my multiplication facts. She wrote them all out on cards and we went over them after dinner. It didn't take long before **I felt overwhelmed** *and frustrated. Multiplication is so hard! I wish I could just use a calculator but mom says it will help me to know them in my head. Every day mom and I went over the cards and after a while I noticed that I was finally starting to learn them! Now when I am doing multiplication in math the answers are so much easier for me. Even though it was hard I am so glad I didn't give up!*

Write about a time when you stuck to something difficult until you succeeded. What happened and how did you feel?

....

....

....

Finishing Off

God, today I am feeling... (Circle or color)

Happy

Blessed

Anxious

Sad

Angry

I feel this way because ....

....

Today I am thankful for ....

Today I am praying for ....

....

Go to page 129 and fill in your "Monthly Mood Tracker" chart.

WEEK THREE
Stick With It

DAY THREE

GROWING ROOTS

Does Jesus understand what it's like to stick with something hard and not give up? Today we will learn that even Jesus got tired at times.

Read:

"This High Priest of ours understands our weaknesses, for he faced all of the same testings we do, yet he did not sin."

Hebrews 4:15 (NLT)

Jesus knew what it was like to have a big job from God. He was sent to Earth to serve God by serving others. He healed the sick, fed the hungry, taught crowds of people, and died on the cross for us. Hebrews 4:15 tells us that Jesus understands when we feel tired because He faced all of the same things we do.

Read:

"Jacob's well was there, and Jesus, tired as he was from the journey, sat down by the well. It was about noon."

John 4:6 (NLT)

If Jesus knew what it was like to feel tired do you think He understands when you are tired and are struggling to stick with things?

 Yes   No

Imagine what would have happened if Jesus had given up on His task and not died on the cross. Would we enjoy the same gift of eternal life today? Whatever job you have may not feel as big as the job Jesus had. But no matter how big or small, it is very important that we learn how to persevere and finish things even when it is hard.

Read:

"For I can do everything through Christ, who gives me strength."

Philippians 4:13 (NLT)

Look at the verse above. Circle the word **everything**.
Where does our strength come from? Write it below.

My strength comes from ·······························

Are you having a hard time sticking with something? On the next page doodle something that you need to "stick" with.

106

In the space below doodle or write something that you need to "stick" with.

Finishing Off

God, today I am feeling... (Circle or color)

Happy

Blessed

Anxious

Sad

Angry

I feel this way because ....

....

Today I am thankful for ....

Today I am praying for ....

....

Go to page 129 and fill in your "Monthly Mood Tracker" chart.

WEEK THREE
Stick With It

Today is: (Color the day of the week)

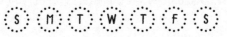

S M T W T F S

DAY FOUR

HARVESTING THE FRUIT

This week we learned about how and why we need to stick with things when they are hard. We learned that God is ready to help us when we ask Him and that we can do all things through Christ who gives us strength (Philippians 4:13).

Why is it important that we do not get into the habit of giving up on things? Why is perseverance so important?

Read:

"Therefore, since we are surrounded by such a huge crowd of witnesses to the life of faith, let us strip off every weight that slows us down, especially the sin that so easily trips us up. And let us run with endurance the race God has set before us. We do this by keeping our eyes on Jesus, the champion who initiates and perfects our faith. Because of the joy awaiting him, he endured the cross, disregarding its shame. Now he is seated in the place of honor beside God's throne."
Hebrews 12:1-2 (NLT)

In Hebrews 12, we read about how the Christian life is a lot like a race. Have you ever watched an Olympic athlete compete in track and field? Olympic athletes will train for 4 years before they are able to compete. During their training years they will often face many obstacles along the way but will need to push through each challenge in order to be successful.

Did you know that when we develop a habit of seeing a task through to the end we are training ourselves to grow spiritually stronger? Just as an athlete will train hard to compete in a race having perseverance in our daily lives will train us to go on to do even bigger things for God! I wonder what God has in store for you? Is it possible He could be training you to persevere through something right now so that you will have the strength to do something amazing for Him in the future?

Look at Hebrews 12:1-2 again.

Who do we need to be keeping our eyes on? Write it below.

....

Let's not miss out on the blessing God has for us when we stick with hard things! Persevere in the little things, do not grow tired in doing good, and watch how God will use your training in the small things to help you do big things for Him someday!

108

Use this space to journal. You can write about what you learned today, your worries, your thoughts, or your prayers.

....

....

....

....

....

....

....

....

....

Finishing Off

God, today I am feeling... (Circle or color)

| Happy | Blessed | Anxious | Sad | Angry |

I feel this way because ....

....

Today I am thankful for ....

Today I am praying for ....

....

Go to page 129 and fill in your "Monthly Mood Tracker" chart.

WEEK THREE
Stick With It

Today is: (Color the day of the week)

S M T W T F S

DAY FIVE

REVIEW AND DISCUSS

What is the hardest thing you have ever done? Why do you think it is important to God that we not give up on things?

....

....

....

....

....

Do you require more perseverance at home, at school, or in your friendships? Write about one task, job, skill, or relationship that you need to "stick" with.

....

....

....

....

....

How have you seen God answer your prayers this week?

....

....

110

CHAPTER TWO, WEEK THREE | STICK WITH IT

Scripture Writing Challenge

Rewrite:
"So let's not get tired of doing what is good. At just the right time we will reap a harvest of blessing if we don't give up."

Galatians 6:9 (NLT)

....

....

....

....

Finishing Off

God, today I am feeling... (Circle or color)

Happy   **Blessed**   **Anxious**   **Sad**   **Angry**

I feel this way because ....

....

Today I am thankful for ....

Today I am praying for ....

....

111

Go to page 129 and fill in your "Monthly Mood Tracker" chart.

Discussion Questions
• Week Three •

Pick one or more questions to discuss with your parents.

Kids ask your parents:

- Describe a big job in your life right now. Do you ever feel tired of that job?
- Have you ever struggled to finish something?
- Have you ever given up on something you wish you had not?

Parents ask your kids:

- Describe a skill, job, or task in your life right now that is really hard.
- Why do you think it is hard to persevere when we fail at something?
- Why do you think it is important to God that we finish what we start?
- How can I pray for you this week?

Family Prayer Requests:

....

....

....

....

Doodles

Use this empty space to draw or doodle!

Week Four
HEAVENLY HELPER

(What is prayer and why is it important?)

WEEK FOUR
Heavenly Helper

Today is: (Color the day of the week)

S M T W T F S

DAY ONE

PLANTING A SEED

Heavenly Helper
(What is prayer and why is it important?)

"Neither height nor depth, nor anything else in all creation, will be able to separate us from the love of God that is in Christ Jesus our Lord."
Romans 8:39 (NIV)

Standing at 418 feet high, the Kingda Ka in Jackson, New Jersey holds the record for being the tallest roller coaster in the world. From extreme heights to extreme drops, Kingda Ka has a reputation of taking people's breath away at every dizzying turn, twist, climb, and drop! Have you ever been to a fair or theme park and experienced the thrill of riding a roller coaster and later wondered how a roller coaster works?

Roller coasters are made up of cars that are connected securely to a track. The roller coaster track will have a strong chain that will pull the cars to the top. Once the coaster reaches the very top the chain will release and the force of gravity will pull the coaster downward at an incredible speed! If you have ever been on a roller coaster you will probably remember feeling your tummy flutter as you screamed the whole way down!

No matter the twists and loops the coaster will take the track securely holds onto the car. Equally important is the job that gravity plays. At all points of the ride, gravity will constantly pull the roller coaster closer towards the track.

So what do roller coasters have to do with being a Christian? More than you probably think! It may surprise you to learn that the life of a Christian can be very similar to a roller coaster. Like a thrilling ride, being a child of God can be so exciting and surprising. We never know what ups or downs, twists, or turns may be up ahead. Similar to how a roller coaster track and the force of gravity work together, God is constantly at work in the life of a believer. In the ups and downs of life, God is always securely holding onto His children. He sent the Holy Spirit as a helper to encourage our hearts and pull us closer to God.

This week we will learn how we can turn to God in every twist and turn of life and how the Holy Spirit helps us.

116

Have you ever been on a roller coaster? How did you feel when the coaster was about the drop?

....

....

....

....

....

....

....

....

....

Finishing Off

God, today I am feeling... (Circle or color)

Happy   Blessed   Anxious   Sad   Angry

I feel this way because ....

....

Today I am thankful for ....

Today I am praying for ....

....

Go to page 129 and fill in your "Monthly Mood Tracker" chart.

Today is: (Color the day of the week)

S M T W T F S

DAY TWO

WATERING FOR GROWTH

Did you know that when Jesus was on Earth He often spent time with children? Jesus LOVED kids and used them as an example when teaching the crowds. Jesus praised how simple kids are. Unlike adults, Jesus saw their wonderful ability to come to Him just as they were.

Read:

"And he took the children in his arms, placed his hands on them and blessed them."

Mark 10:16 (NLT)

Can you imagine what it would have been like to see Jesus face to face? What an amazing experience that would have been! I imagine that even the most thrilling roller coaster could not come close to comparing how the children felt when Jesus blessed them.

We may not have Jesus with us on Earth anymore but just as Jesus welcomed the children with wide open arms He still welcomes His children to come to Him in prayer, no matter what. He loves it when children talk to Him in prayer.

Read:

" Because of Christ and our faith in him, we can now come boldly and confidently into God's presence."

Ephesians 3:12 (NLT)

Underline or circle the words **boldly** and **confidently**. What does it mean to come into God's presence boldly and confidently? It means that because of Jesus you can talk to God about anything without having to feel ashamed or afraid.

Coming to Jesus means that you can talk to Him any time, any place. You can talk to Him in the car, when you are at school, at home, or even when you are awake at night and can't sleep.

Read:

"He will not let you stumble; the one who watches over you will not slumber."

Psalm 121:3 (NLT)

Aren't you so glad that God never sleeps? He is always there when we need to talk to Him. Tomorrow we will learn about why prayer is important.

My best friend moved away last year. We used to see each other almost every day. It has been really hard not being able to talk to him like I used to. His house is in a different time zone so calling him can be tricky. When I am getting home from school he is getting ready for bed. When I have a bad day or even when I have a good day I often wish I could talk to him. Even though it has been hard not having my best friend close my dad has taught me how to talk to God instead. He tells me that **God loves hearing from me and is always available** to listen. I am thankful that God is never too busy to talk to. He is always there for me no matter what time it is.

Write about a time when you were thankful you could talk to God.

....

....

....

Finishing Off

God, today I am feeling... (Circle or color)

Happy

Blessed

Anxious

Sad

Angry

I feel this way because ....

....

Today I am thankful for ....

Today I am praying for ....

....

119

Go to page 129 and fill in your "Monthly Mood Tracker" chart.

Today is: (Color the day of the week)

(S) (M) (T) (W) (T) (F) (S)

DAY THREE

GROWING ROOTS

A couple days ago we learned that the Christian life can be similar to a roller coaster full of ups and downs. Have you ever been on a roller coaster? Was it at a theme park or a fair? Write about your experience below.

....

....

Have you ever had a day that started off great then took a turn for the worst? It is true that life can bring unexpected twists and turns, highs, and lows. We also learned that no matter what we face God never lets go of us.

What does God expect from us when things are good and when things are bad?

Read:

"I will praise the Lord at all times. I will constantly speak his praises."
Psalm 34:1 (NLT)

Circle the phrase **at all times.**
According to the very first sentence in the verse above, when does God want us to praise Him? When things are good? When things are bad? Fill in the blank.

God wants me to praise Him ....

Read:

"Don't worry about anything; instead, pray about everything. Tell God what you need, and thank him for all he has done."
Philippians 4:6 (NLT)

What does God tell us to do when we worry?
Circle the words **tell** and **thank.**

In the two verses we looked at today we learned that prayer is not just about telling God what we want. He is not a genie in a magical lamp ready to grant us our every wish. Prayer is so much more than that! Prayer is how we grow in our relationship with God. When we come to Him and thank Him for His many blessings and share with Him our worries and requests we show Him that we love Him for who He is, not just for what He can give us.

Tomorrow we will learn about what the Holy Spirit's role is when we pray.

120

Doodle something you are thankful for!

Finishing Off

God, today I am feeling... (Circle or color)

Happy

Blessed

Anxious

Sad

Angry

I feel this way because ....

....

Today I am thankful for ....

Today I am praying for ....

....

Go to page 129 and fill in your "Monthly Mood Tracker" chart.

WEEK FOUR
Heavenly Helper

Today is: (Color the day of the week)

S M T W T F S

DAY FOUR

HARVESTING THE FRUIT

Have you ever felt like you wanted to talk to God and didn't know what to say? Maybe you felt like you might mess up or say the wrong thing or that He wouldn't hear you.

Read:

"And when you pray, do not heap up empty phrases as the Gentiles do, for they think that they will be heard for their many words. Do not be like them, for your Father knows what you need before you ask him."

Matthew 6:7-8 (ESV)

Jesus told His disciples in Matthew 6 that God is not impressed by how well we can pray or how long our prayers are. Prayer does not have to be fancy. God is more interested in our hearts than how fancy our prayers are. Our prayers can be as simple as, "Thank you God for your blessings!" or "God I feel scared, please help me" or "I am worried about somebody, can you help?"

Our prayers may be really short and very simple and that is OK! God does not need long prayers, He just wants to hear from us.

Read:

"But the Helper, the Holy Spirit, whom the Father will send in my name, he will teach you all things and bring to your remembrance all that I have said to you."

John 14:26 (NKJV)

Circle the words **Helper** and **Holy Spirit**.

Did you know that we have a Holy Spirit helper?
The Holy Spirit is the greatest gift we have ever been given. He is constantly helping us, pulling our hearts closer to God. He even prays for us when we don't have the right words.

Read:

"And the Holy Spirit helps us in our weakness. For example, we don't know what God wants us to pray for. But the Holy Spirit prays for us with groanings that cannot be expressed in words."

Romans 8:26 (NLT)

Aren't you so blessed to know that even in our prayers God is helping us? On the next page, write out a short prayer to God thanking Him for the gift of the Holy Spirit.

122

You have a **Holy Spirit** helper praying for you. **Write** out a prayer to God thanking **Him** for the gift of the Holy Spirit.

....

....

....

....

....

....

....

....

....

Finishing Off

God, today I am feeling... (Circle or color)

Happy   Blessed   Anxious   Sad   Angry

I feel this way because ....

....

Today I am thankful for ....

Today I am praying for ....

....

123

Go to page 129 and fill in your "Monthly Mood Tracker" chart.

WEEK FOUR
Heavenly Helper

DAY FIVE

REVIEW AND DISCUSS

Have you ever felt like life was a lot like a roller coaster? Write out some of your greatest highs and lows.

....

....

....

....

....

This week you learned that God loves it when children come to Him in prayer. He loves to hear about the good and the bad stuff and He wants us to praise Him at all times. He does not expect fancy words when we pray. Think about your prayer life right now. In what ways can you improve your prayer time?

....

....

....

....

How have you seen God answer your prayers this week?

....

....

124

Scripture Writing Challenge

Rewrite:

"Neither height nor depth, nor anything else in all creation, will be able to separate us from the love of God that is in Christ Jesus our Lord."

Romans 8:39 (NIV)

....

....

....

....

Finishing Off

God, today I am feeling... (Circle or color)

Happy   Blessed   Anxious   Sad   Angry

I feel this way because ....

....

Today I am thankful for ....

Today I am praying for ....

....

Go to page 129 and fill in your "Monthly Mood Tracker" chart.

Discussion Questions

• Week Four •

Pick one or more questions to discuss with your parents.

Kids ask your parents:

- Have you ever been on a roller coaster? Do you know how a roller coaster works? (If not, go to page 116 and read the second paragraph).
- Do you find it easier to pray when things are good or bad?

Parents ask your kids:

- What did you learn about how God feels about children?
- What did you learn about prayer this week?
- Do you usually pray more during the highs or lows of life?
- How can I pray for you?

Family Prayer Requests:

....

....

....

Doodles

Use this empty space to draw or doodle!

MONTHLY MOOD

TRACKER
CHAPTER TWO

Color a dot under how you are feeling today.

Angry

○ ○ ○ ○ ○
○ ○ ○ ○ ○
○ ○ ○ ○ ○
○ ○ ○ ○ ○

Sad

○ ○ ○ ○ ○
○ ○ ○ ○ ○
○ ○ ○ ○ ○
○ ○ ○ ○ ○

Anxious

○ ○ ○ ○ ○
○ ○ ○ ○ ○
○ ○ ○ ○ ○
○ ○ ○ ○ ○

Blessed

○ ○ ○ ○ ○
○ ○ ○ ○ ○
○ ○ ○ ○ ○
○ ○ ○ ○ ○

Happy

○ ○ ○ ○ ○
○ ○ ○ ○ ○
○ ○ ○ ○ ○
○ ○ ○ ○ ○

CHAPTER 2 MOOD TRACKER CHART

Chapter Three
GOD GUIDES

"The Lord says, 'I will guide you along the best pathway
for your life. I will advise you and watch over you.'"

Psalm 32:8 (NLT)

Week One

THE RIGHT STEPS

(How can I love others?)

WEEK ONE
The
Right Steps

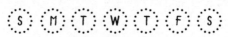

Today is: (Color the day of the week)

S M T W T F S

DAY ONE

PLANTING A SEED

The Right Steps
(How can I love others?)

"Dear friends, let us continue to love one another, for love comes from God. Anyone who loves is a child of God and knows God."
1 John 4:7 (NLT)

Flour, eggs, milk, sugar, baking soda, butter, and definitely piles of chocolate chips! These are some of the ingredients you will often reach for when you are getting ready to bake something sweet.

Have you ever baked chocolate chip cookies on a Saturday morning with your mom, dad, or a sibling? Baking can be a lot of fun and can be a great way to enjoy some quality time with the people you love. It is pretty awesome to be able to create a sweet-tasting treat out of a pile of simple ingredients. When done right, baking can result in a delicious treat enjoyed by everyone.

Anyone who has baked at least once in their lifetime will know that it takes the right steps with the right ingredients to be successful. That is where a recipe comes in! A recipe can tell you what you need, how much, and in what order to make your baking successful. Have you ever made a batch of cookies and when you tasted them noticed right away that something was not right? Maybe you forgot to add enough sugar, added too much salt, or you used baking soda instead of baking powder. Some of the most common baking fails will come from not following the recipe correctly.

When it comes to our relationships many times we can be guilty of the same mistakes. God has given us a clear recipe for how to love our friends and family but we can get off track and forget some of the most important ingredients.

Luckily, we have an ultimate recipe we can follow. The Bible has a lot to say about love. God has shown us in the Bible how to follow His example of love. When we do, we will enjoy the result of enjoying sweet relationships.

This week we will learn how to love others by following God's example and what ingredients are key to making our relationships successful.

134

Use this space to journal. You can write about what you learned today, your worries, your thoughts, or your prayers.

....

....

....

....

....

....

....

Finishing Off

God, today I am feeling... (Circle or color)

Happy   Blessed   Anxious   Sad   Angry

I feel this way because ....

....

Today I am thankful for ....

Today I am praying for ....

....

Go to page 189 and fill in your "Monthly Mood Tracker" chart.

WEEK ONE
The
Right Steps

Today is: (Color the day of the week)

S   M   T   W   T   F   S

DAY TWO

WATERING FOR GROWTH

Yesterday we learned that God guides us in
our relationships by giving us His Word
as a recipe for love.

Today we are going to look at two ingredients needed to enjoy sweet
relationships with our friends and family.

Read:
"Love is patient, love is kind. It does not envy, it does not boast, it is not proud."
1 Corinthians 13:4 (NLT)

Circle the words **patient** and **kind**.

Patience and kindness are two love ingredients that go hand-in-hand. Think of icing and
sprinkles! Sweet to the taste, patience and kindness is a sweet response when someone
frustrates or disappoints us.

How do you usually respond when your sibling(s) annoy you? Or when your mom is
asking you to do a chore you don't want to do? Are you patient enough to wait your turn
when playing a game with a friend? Are you kind when someone isn't kind to you?

Read:
"Don't you see how wonderfully kind, tolerant, and patient God is with you? Does this mean
nothing to you? Can't you see that his kindness is intended to turn you from your sin?"
Romans 2:4 (NLT)

Again, circle the word **patient**.
Now look at the next four words after that. Is God patient towards you?

Aren't you so thankful that God is patient with us? How can you be the same for those
around you?

Read:
"Be kind to one another, tenderhearted, forgiving one another, as God in Christ forgave you."
Ephesians 4:32 (ESV)

Have you ever blown it big time but were treated with kindness and forgiveness anyway?
Giving kindness when we don't deserve it is what God does best. God shows us how to be
patient and loving towards those around us by reminding us of how
patient and kind He is with us. How can you begin to show
more kindness and patience to others today?

136

On Sundays our family likes to play board games. We each take turns picking the game. This time my brother got to pick and he chose his favorite game. He always picks the SAME game! The only reason he picks it is because he always wins. Just like I thought would happen, my brother won the game (again!) and when he said, "Good game!" I ignored him and stormed off. I know that losing is not a big deal but **I felt so mad**. Little brothers can be so annoying! My mom made me come back and apologize for being a poor sport. The next week it was my turn to pick the game and this time I won. Instead of being a poor sport my brother gave me a high-five and said, "Nice job!" I felt so guilty. I think I have a lot to learn.

Think of someone in your life you are having a hard time being patient and kind with. How can God's example begin to change how you treat that person?

....

....

Finishing Off

God, today I am feeling... (Circle or color)

Happy

Blessed

Anxious

Sad

Angry

I feel this way because ....

....

Today I am thankful for ....

Today I am praying for ....

....

Go to page 189 and fill in your "Monthly Mood Tracker" chart.

Today is: (Color the day of the week)

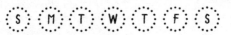

S · M · T · W · T · F · S

DAY THREE
GROWING ROOTS

Yesterday we learned the first two ingredients we need to enjoy sweet relationships. Today we will learn about the ingredients we will want to avoid if we hope to have good relationships with others.

Read:

"Love is patient and kind. Love is not jealous or boastful or proud or rude. It does not demand its own way. It is not irritable, and it keeps no record of being wronged."

1 Corinthians 13:4-5 (NLT)

This verse also tells us what love is NOT, there are four. Circle **jealous**, **boastful**, **proud**, and **rude**.

Have you ever been jealous of something someone else has? Maybe it is a vacation they get to enjoy, a new toy, or gadget. Have you ever been jealous of other people's gifts and abilities? Maybe you have a hard time not feeling jealous when grades come easily to a friend while you work hard and still barely make passing grades.

Jealousy can create feelings of anger and bitterness and can lead to us not being thankful for what God has given us. God took jealousy so seriously that He included it in the Ten Commandments when He said not to covet (want) what other people have (Exodus 20:17). When jealousy creeps in it will always spoil our relationships. We saw this on page 28 when we read about Joseph's brothers being so jealous of him that they sold him into slavery (Genesis 37:11,18).

Think back to a time when you felt jealous of a sibling or friend. If jealousy is the opposite of being grateful, what was it that you were ungrateful for?

I was jealous of ....

because I wasn't grateful for ....

Maybe you don't struggle with jealousy but you tend to brag about the things you have. When you get something new or accomplish something difficult is your first response to make sure everyone knows? No one enjoys being around someone who always brags. Bragging can be a sign that we don't realize that the things, gifts, and abilities we have come from God, not from ourselves. When we brag to others we are being rude.

Read:

"Let someone else praise you, not your own mouth - a stranger, not your own lips."

Proverbs 27:2 (NLT)

According to this verse is bragging OK? What do you think is the difference between being happy about our blessings or accomplishments, and bragging? Write your thoughts on the next page.

138

What do you think is the difference between being happy about your blessings or accomplishments, and bragging about them?

....

....

....

....

....

....

....

....

Finishing Off

God, today I am feeling... (Circle or color)

Happy   **Blessed**   **Anxious**   **Sad**   **Angry**

I feel this way because ....

....

Today I am thankful for ....

Today I am praying for ....

....

Go to page 189 and fill in your "Monthly Mood Tracker" chart.

WEEK ONE
The Right Steps

Today is: (Color the day of the week)

S M T W T F S

DAY FOUR

HARVESTING THE FRUIT

Read:

"Love is patient and kind. Love is not jealous or boastful or proud or rude. It does not demand its own way. It is not irritable, and it keeps no record of being wronged."

1 Corinthians 13:4-5 (NLT)

Circle the phrases **not irritable** and **keeps no record of being wronged**.

Have you ever heard of "waking up on the wrong side of the bed?" We all have days when we start the day off feeling grumpy. It can be for no specific reason other than we just feel "off." When we have days like this it's very easy to get angry over little things and snap at the people we love the most.

Read:

"And 'don't sin by letting anger control you.' Don't let the sun go down while you are still angry."

Ephesians 4:26 (NLT)

Have a look at this verse. Does it say that you are never allowed to be angry?

It is normal to feel angry sometimes. The Bible tells us to not let anger control us and cause us to sin. Anger that causes us to snap at someone is harmful and can create problems in our relationships. "Don't let the sun go down while you are sill angry" means to quickly control your anger before it takes control of you.

Read:

"A hot-tempered person starts fights; a cool-tempered person stops them."

Proverbs 15:18 (NLT)

Have you ever felt so angry you felt like you were going to explode? Proverbs 15:18 tells us that a hot tempered person starts a fight and a cool tempered person stops them. When you feel anger starting to flare up what can you do to cool off before you do or say something you might regret?

Read:

"Lord, if you kept a record of our sins, who, O Lord, could ever survive? But you offer forgiveness that we might learn to fear you."

Psalm 130:3-4 (NLT)

Do you tend to remind people about the mistakes they have made in the past? Or are you quick to forgive and move on? How can God's example of how He treats your mistakes help you to respond more lovingly to those around you?

THREE, WEEK ONE | THE RIGHT STEPS

Flip through the last few weeks of your book. On the days you recorded you were angry, what was the reason for your anger? How did you handle that anger? Is there anyone you need to apologize to? Journal your thoughts below.

....

....

....

....

....

....

....

....

....

....

Finishing Off

God, today I am feeling... (Circle or color)

Happy   Blessed   Anxious   Sad   Angry

I feel this way because ....

....

Today I am thankful for ....

Today I am praying for ....

....

Go to page 189 and fill in your "Monthly Mood Tracker" chart.

WEEK ONE
The
Right Steps

Today is: (Color the day of the week)

S M T W T F S

DAY FIVE

REVIEW AND DISCUSS

What is your favorite thing to bake? Have you ever baked something and had it completely fail? Write about your experience below.

....

....

....

....

....

This week you saw the ingredients for sweet relationships. You also learned what love is not. What challenged you the most this week? What areas do you need growth in your family relationships and friendships?

....

....

....

....

....

How have you seen God answer your prayers this week?

....

....

142

Scripture Writing Challenge

Rewrite:

"Dear friends, let us continue to love one another, for love comes from God. Anyone who loves is a child of God and knows God."

1 John 4:7 (NLT)

....

....

....

....

Finishing Off

God, today I am feeling... (Circle or color)

Happy

Blessed

Anxious

Sad

Angry

I feel this way because ....

....

Today I am thankful for ....

Today I am praying for ....

....

Go to page 189 and fill in your "Monthly Mood Tracker" chart.

Discussion Questions

• Week One •

Pick one or more questions to discuss with your parents.

Kids ask your parents:

- Do you ever struggle with being patient and kind?
- Have you ever lost your temper at a friend and had to apologize?
- How do I usually treat others when I am frustrated?

Parents ask your kids:

- How are your friendships going right now?
- Are you being kind and patient towards others?
- What did you learn about how God treats us?
- What do you think is the difference between bragging and being happy about something? (Share what you wrote on page 139).

Family Prayer Requests:

....

....

....

....

Doodles

Use this empty space to draw or doodle!

Week Two
AN HONEST GUIDE
(What is integrity?)

WEEK TWO
An Honest Guide

Today is: (Color the day of the week)

(S) (M) (T) (W) (T) (F) (S)

DAY ONE

PLANTING A SEED

An Honest Guide
(What is integrity?)

"Behold, you delight in truth in the inward being, and you teach me wisdom in the secret heart."
Psalm 51:6 (ESV)

New Year's, Easter, and Christmas are all holidays that many cultures celebrate. These dates are well known and in most calendars. But have you ever heard of National Opposite Day? Celebrated every year on January 25th, Opposite Day is a day where those celebrating must do everything backwards!

Good morning is good night, hello is goodbye, dinner is breakfast and breakfast dinner, up is down and down is up. Anything you can think of that has an opposite is fair game on Opposite Day!

It could be a fun game to play for a time but could you imagine how chaotic life would be if everyone constantly lived this way? It would be hard to take anyone seriously if everything they said and did was not what they actually meant. It would become impossible to trust anyone!

Jesus spoke about this topic in Matthew 5. He said, "Let your yes be yes and your no be no." (Matthew 5:37). He was trying to teach His disciples that keeping their word was important. He wanted them to know that they should avoid making an oath or promise without following through on what they said they would do. Jesus wanted them to be men who were trustworthy and honest — even when it was difficult. Jesus wanted them to be men of integrity.

Nothing has changed since Jesus' time. Our actions and our words are an important part of integrity. When we do the opposite of what we say we are going to do, or don't follow through on a promise we have made our integrity is damaged and it hurts the heart of God. Since God is a God who is not slow in keeping His promises to us He instructs us to do the same for others in our lives.

So when January 25th comes along, enjoy some Opposite Day fun! Eat breakfast for dinner, or wear your clothes backwards to school and see if anyone notices. Eat dessert first (if your parents say it's OK!), or even try eating dinner with the opposite hand! Enjoy some silly fun by doing the opposite of what people expect. But when it comes to your word—be a person who follows through on what they say. Be a kid of integrity.

148

Use this space to journal. You can write about what you learned today, your worries, your thoughts, or your prayers.

....

....

....

....

....

....

....

....

....

Finishing Off

God, today I am feeling... (Circle or color)

Happy　　**Blessed**　　**Anxious**　　**Sad**　　**Angry**

I feel this way because ....

....

Today I am thankful for ....

Today I am praying for ....

....

Go to page 189 and fill in your "Monthly Mood Tracker" chart.

WEEK TWO
An Honest Guide

Today is: (Color the day of the week)

S M T W T F S

DAY TWO

WATERING FOR GROWTH

Yesterday we learned about being a kid of integrity.
Keeping our promises and following through on what we
say we are going to do is a big part of having integrity.

Read:

"It is better to say nothing than to make a promise and not keep it."
Ecclesiastes 5:5 (NLT)

and

Read:

"Just say a simple, 'Yes, I will,' or 'No, I won't.' Anything beyond this is from the evil one."
Matthew 5:37 (NLT)

Have you ever promised your mom you would clean your room only to pick up the remote and flip on the TV instead? Have you ever promised a friend you would attend their birthday party and got another invitation to a better party on the same day? Have you ever given something away then asked for it back? Or said you would help a friend then changed your mind?

The Bible says that it is better to not say anything at all than to make a promise and not follow through on it. When we stick to our word people know they can trust us and that we will do what we said we would do.

Would people say you are a kid of your word? Why or why not?

Read:

"The Lord is not slow in keeping his promise, as some understand slowness. Instead he is patient with you, not wanting anyone to perish, but everyone to come to repentance."
2 Peter 3:9 (NIV)

Circle the phrase **not slow**.
This verse tells us that God does not promise us something then drag it out or put us off saying, "I'll get to that later!" When God promises us something He keeps His Word. The great news is that even when we fail to keep our promises to others, God never fails to keep His promises to us.

150

I am so excited! When I was at youth group tonight our pastor told us that next weekend he is planning a super fun father-son camping trip! All the boys and their dads are invited. When we got home I told my dad about it and asked if we could go but he reminded me that I had already agreed to help my friend with a science project that same weekend. **I am so bummed out!** I know I gave my word but a camping trip sounds like so much more fun.

Write about a time when you had to keep your word even when it was difficult. What happened?

....

....

....

Finishing Off

God, today I am feeling... (Circle or color)

Happy   Blessed   Anxious   Sad   Angry

I feel this way because ....

....

Today I am thankful for ....

Today I am praying for ....

....

Go to page 189 and fill in your "Monthly Mood Tracker" chart.

WEEK TWO
An Honest Guide

Today is: (Color the day of the week)
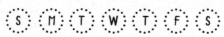
S · M · T · W · T · F · S

DAY THREE
GROWING ROOTS

Having integrity starts with keeping our word to others. But having integrity also means telling the truth especially to those we love the most.

Read:
"The Lord detests lying lips, but he delights in those who tell the truth."
Proverbs 12:22 (NLT)

Circle the phrase **lying lips**.
The definition of lying means to speak something that is not true on purpose. Proverbs 12:22 says that the Lord delights in those who tell the truth. The Bible tells us that God tells the truth (Psalm 33:4). When we do not follow His example of honesty we can hurt others and ourselves. Since God loves us so much He wants to spare us the hurt that comes from lying.

Read:
"For the Scriptures say, 'If you want to enjoy life and see many happy days, keep your tongue from speaking evil and your lips from telling lies.'"
1 Peter 3:10 (NLT)

Do you see a promise in this verse?

Underline the phrase **enjoy life and see many happy days**.
God promises that when we do not lie we will enjoy the blessing of a rich and happy life. God loves us so deeply He knows the trouble that we can cause by lying to our family or our friends. Lies have a way of starting off small then getting bigger and bigger. Lies separate us from those we love the most and make us untrustworthy. But God wants better for us. God's desire is for us to enjoy honest relationships with our family and friends.

Read:
"An honest answer is like a kiss of friendship."
Proverbs 24:26 (NLT)

Is there anyone in your life whom you admire for being a person who is honest? If so, write their name below.

I admire .... because they tell the truth.

We learned last week that God is patient and kind to us. He gives us so many chances. He knows that we will not always make good choices but He also wants us to enjoy happy days by being honest with those around us. On the next page draw a picture of the person you admire for being a person who tells the truth.

152

Doodle a picture of someone you admire because they tell the truth.

Finishing Off

God, today I am feeling... (Circle or color)

Happy   Blessed   Anxious   Sad   Angry

I feel this way because ....

....

Today I am thankful for ....

Today I am praying for ....

....

153

Go to page 189 and fill in your "Monthly Mood Tracker" chart.

WEEK TWO
An Honest Guide

Today is: (Color the day of the week)

S M T W T F S

DAY FOUR

HARVESTING THE FRUIT

What does being sneaky about our sin have to do with not being a person of integrity? Today we will look at two people in the Bible named Ananias and his wife Sapphira who were sneaky. They tried to hide their sin of taking money that didn't belong to them.

Read:

"But there was a certain man named Ananias who, with his wife, Sapphira, sold some property. He brought part of the money to the apostles, claiming it was the full amount. With his wife's consent, he kept the rest. Then Peter said, 'Ananias, why have you let Satan fill your heart? You lied to the Holy Spirit, and you kept some of the money for yourself.'"

Acts 5:1-3 (NLT)

Have you ever been tempted to be sneaky and take something that wasn't yours? Ananias and his wife cheated by selling property and keeping some of the money for themselves when it should have gone to the Apostles. They tried to hide their sin from the Apostles.

Ananias and Sapphira were caught in their deceit and it didn't end very well for them. But what about lies that no one ever finds out about? Have you ever cheated on a test and never told anyone? Or cheated in a game and won but kept silent? Have you ever tricked your sibling out of something that was theirs? Or took an extra snack when your mom told you "No"?

Read:

"God would surely have known it, for he knows the secrets of every heart."

Psalm 44:21 (NLT)

The Bible tells us that God knows every secret of the heart. Even when we try to be sneaky and hide our sin from others, God sees it.

Read:

"Behold, you delight in truth in the inward being, and you teach me wisdom in the secret heart."

Psalm 51:6 (ESV)

Look at the Psalm 51:6 above. Underline the phrase **you teach me wisdom.**

God wants to teach us how to be wise. When we are not sneaky about our sin but instead are honest, God will teach us how to become kids of integrity.

Have you ever been sneaky about a sin and never got caught? Is there someone you need to talk to today to make it right? Journal your thoughts on the next page.

154

Have you ever been sneaky about a sin and never been caught? Do you need to talk to someone today to make it right? Journal your thoughts below.

....

....

....

....

....

....

....

....

....

Finishing Off

God, today I am feeling... (Circle or color)

Happy   Blessed   Anxious   Sad   Angry

I feel this way because ....

....

Today I am thankful for ....

Today I am praying for ....

....

Go to page 189 and fill in your "Monthly Mood Tracker" chart.

WEEK TWO
An Honest Guide

Today is: (Color the day of the week)

S M T W T F S

DAY FIVE
REVIEW AND DISCUSS

Write about a time when you were tempted to tell a lie but didn't, or told a lie and regretted it. What happened and how did you feel?

....

....

....

....

....

This week you learned about following through when you say you are going to do something. Do you think others would say that you are a kid who keeps their word?

....

....

....

....

....

How have you seen God answer your prayers this week?

....

....

156

Scripture Writing Challenge

Rewrite:
"Behold, you delight in truth in the inward being, and you teach me wisdom in the secret heart."
Psalm 51:6 (ESV)

....

....

....

....

Finishing Off

God, today I am feeling... (Circle or color)

Happy   Blessed   Anxious   Sad   Angry

I feel this way because ....

....

Today I am thankful for ....

Today I am praying for ....

....

Go to page 189 and fill in your "Monthly Mood Tracker" chart.

Discussion Questions

• Week Two •

Pick one or more questions to discuss with your parents.

Kids ask your parents:

- In what ways am I a kid of integrity?
- When you were a kid did you ever do something bad then try to hide it?
- How am I at keeping my word?

Parents ask your kids:

- Do you find it hard to stick to your word?
- What did you learn from the story of Ananias and Sapphira? What mistake did they make?
- Is there any sin that God does not see?

Family Prayer Requests:

....

....

....

....

Doodles

Use this empty space to draw or doodle!

Week Three
THIS IS THE WAY

(How can I make good choices?)

Today is: (Color the day of the week)

S M T W T F S

DAY ONE

PLANTING A SEED

This is the Way
(How can I make good choices?)

*"Whether you turn to the right or to the left, your ears will hear a voice behind you saying,
'This is the way; walk in it.' "*
Isaiah 30:21 (NIV)

In the summer, people of all ages will fill their backpacks with snacks and water and head out to their favorite hiking trails to enjoy the smell of fresh trees and the sound of birds chirping. Going for a family hike can be a great way to get outside and enjoy the fresh air. Away from the hustle and bustle of the city hiking can bring a different kind of adventure!

But did you also know that hiking isn't always a fun experience? In fact, every year hundreds of people will veer off a trail by accident and find themselves unable to find their way back. What began as a desire to take a closer look at an interesting insect or even snap a photo of some wildflowers can turn into a frightening realization that the path you were once following has suddenly disappeared. Without a compass or a map telling them where to go; a hiker can find themselves in a very serious situation. A compass is a very important tool that could be the difference between a hiker staying lost for a very long time or quickly finding the right path again.

People in Bible times knew a lot about navigating the outdoors. The children of Israel wandered for 40 years before coming into the Promised Land. Even Jesus Himself spent a large part of His life in the wilderness, it was there that Satan tempted Jesus for 40 days (Matthew 4: 1-11).

The activity of hiking can be very similar to our lives. Sometimes the path we are on can seem right to us but very quickly we can be tempted to turn away from the right path and follow a path that could be bad for us. Without a compass directing us it can be hard to know which way to turn to get back on track.

In Isaiah 30:21, God lovingly promises to bless His people by guiding them towards what is right and warning them of what is wrong. God's promise to guide us is still the same today. When temptation tells us to veer off the right path He points us to the ultimate compass — the Bible — to show us the right way to get us back on track.

So the next time your family is packing for a hike don't forget to bring a compass and next time you face a hard decision and don't know which way to go, make sure you check your spiritual compass—God's Word. In it, you will know how to get back to God's perfect path for you.

162

Does your family enjoy hiking? Write about your favorite memory of a family hike.

....

....

....

....

....

....

....

....

Finishing Off

God, today I am feeling... (Circle or color)

Happy   Blessed   Anxious   Sad   Angry

I feel this way because ....

....

Today I am thankful for ....

Today I am praying for ....

....

Go to page 189 and fill in your "Monthly Mood Tracker" chart.

Today is: (Color the day of the week)

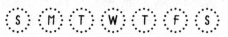

(S) (M) (T) (W) (T) (F) (S)

DAY TWO

WATERING FOR GROWTH

You've heard it said, "Just follow your heart!" This popular phrase is in movies, on t-shirts, notebooks, and a main theme throughout children's books.

But what if the heart can be lied to? What if our hearts can lead us away from God's best for us? Have you ever made a decision based on your feelings; only to find out you were wrong? You aren't alone!

Read:

"The human heart is the most deceitful of all things, and desperately wicked. Who really knows how bad it is?"

Jeremiah 17:9 (NLT)

Circle the words **deceitful** and **wicked**. According to this verse, can our hearts be trusted?

 Yes   **No**

To "follow your heart" really means to allow our feelings to decide what is right and wrong.

On the next page, journal about a time when you made a choice based only on your feelings. How did it go? What happened?

Read:

"My conscience is clear, but that doesn't prove I'm right. It is the Lord himself who will examine me and decide."

1 Corinthians 4:4 (NLT)

Our feelings are an important part of our lives. They reveal our joy and happiness and can protect us from harm. However, the Bible also tells us that the heart is desperately wicked and can not be trusted to make good choices. 1 Corinthians 4:4 also says that we can make choices that we feel good about but are actually wrong.

So how can we know what is the right path and the wrong path? How can you make good choices that honor God?

Read:

"Trust in the Lord with all your heart, and do not lean on your own understanding. In all your ways acknowledge him, and he will make straight your paths."

Proverbs 3:5-6 (NIV)

Circle the phrase **in all your ways acknowledge him.**

The word "acknowledge" means to know God personally. Yesterday, we learned that the Bible is our ultimate compass that directs us. When we get to know God by reading the Bible we are less likely to follow our hearts and more likely to follow the straight path He has for us. God's path is always the right one.

164

*Over the summer we moved to a new town. The first few weeks were really lonely but then I met a group of girls who were really nice to me. They complimented my hair and clothes and said that I was cool enough to be part of their group. But people around town say that my new friends are bad because they get into trouble. These girls are nice to me and it **felt really good** to have friends again. The other day my new friends wanted me to sneak into a movie with them. They told me that they did it all the time and had never been caught. Suddenly, I realized that everyone was right about my new friends. I didn't want to listen when people warned me but now I see that I made a wrong choice.*

Have you ever been tempted to follow your heart? What happened?

....

....

Finishing Off

God, today I am feeling... (Circle or color)

 Happy   Blessed   Anxious   Sad   Angry

I feel this way because ....

....

Today I am thankful for ....

Today I am praying for ....

....

Go to page 189 and fill in your "Monthly Mood Tracker" chart.

WEEK THREE
This is the Way

Today is: (Color the day of the week)

S M T W T F S

DAY THREE

GROWING ROOTS

Have you ever eaten a ton of junk food and felt sick afterwards? The things we allow into our stomach will either help or hurt our ability to grow strong and healthy. This is also true spiritually.

Although our hearts can't be fully trusted we still need to make sure that the things we allow into our hearts will help us grow strong and healthy spiritually.

Read:
"Guard your heart above all else, for it determines the course of your life."
Proverbs 4:23 (NLT)

Circle the word **guard**.
Why do you think it is important to guard our hearts? Journal your thoughts below.

....

....

Read:
"Don't be fooled by those who say such things, for 'bad company corrupts good character.'"
1 Corinthians 15:33 (NLT)

Circle the phrase **bad company corrupts.**

Think about the story you read yesterday about the girl who followed a group of girls she shouldn't have. Proverbs 12:26 tells us "The righteous choose their friends carefully..." When we choose friends who are disrespectful to adults, who use bad language, or consistently gossip we can be sure that their behavior will start to affect our actions and behavior too.

"Bad company" can also take other forms such as the books we read, shows we watch, or even the music we listen to. All of these things will influence our hearts towards God or away from Him.

Guarding our hearts means that we are careful to choose our company wisely knowing that our hearts play a big part in how we behave. Are your choices in friendships, TV shows, movies, music, or books helping or hurting your ability to grow strong spiritually? Are you guarding your heart?

Focus this week on making healthy heart choices that will honor God.

166

Doodle a picture of your favorite television show. Do you think it is a good or bad choice? Does your favorite show honor God?

Finishing Off

God, today I am feeling... *(Circle or color)*

Happy

Blessed

Anxious

Sad

Angry

I feel this way because ....

....

Today I am thankful for ....

Today I am praying for ....

....

167

Go to page 189 and fill in your "Monthly Mood Tracker" chart.

Today is: (Color the day of the week)

S M T W T F S

DAY FOUR

HARVESTING THE FRUIT

All of us at some point will make choices that will lead us away from God's best for us. We will say something we regret, hurt someone we love, or do something we know is not right. Mistakes are a part of being human and God knows that we will not always make the right choices. When you realize you have chosen a wrong path what can you do to make it right?

Read:

"But if we confess our sins to him, he is faithful and just to forgive us our sins and to cleanse us from all wickedness."

1 John 1:9 (NLT)

Circle the phrase **confess our sins to him.**

In order to find the right path again we first need to recognize that we have gotten off track in the first place! To confess simply means to admit to God when we mess up. A quick prayer such as, "God I really blew it, please forgive me" is a simple and honest prayer of confession. Notice that God's forgiveness immediately follows.

The second way to get back on the right path again is to realize that our mistake may have hurt someone and to make it right with that person.

Read:

"Confess your sins to each other and pray for each other so that you may be healed. The earnest prayer of a righteous person has great power and produces wonderful results."

James 5:16 (NLT)

Circle the phrase **confess.**

God loves seeing us enjoy relationship with those around us. Part of keeping those relationships strong is by making sure we are quick to apologize when we hurt others. Asking for forgiveness from someone we have hurt can bring instant healing to a relationship.

If you have asked for God's forgiveness and the forgiveness of the person you hurt, the Bible says there is one more thing to do: move on!

Read:

"Brothers and sisters, I do not consider myself yet to have taken hold of it. But one thing I do: Forgetting what is behind and straining toward what is ahead"

Philippians 3:13 (NIV)

God does not want us to keep going back to where we got off track. As we learned earlier, making mistakes and seeking forgiveness is a lifelong process! Did you know that even your parents get off track too?

If you have taken steps to confess and apologize then it's time to keep walking forward. God does not want you staying stuck, He has better things for you up ahead.

Use this space to journal. You can write about what you learned today, your worries, your thoughts, or your prayers.

....

....

....

....

....

....

....

....

....

Finishing Off

God, today I am feeling... (Circle or color)

Happy   Blessed   Anxious   Sad   Angry

I feel this way because ....

....

Today I am thankful for ....

Today I am praying for ....

....

169

Go to page 189 and fill in your "Monthly Mood Tracker" chart.

WEEK THREE
This is the Way

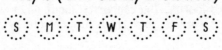

Today is: (Color the day of the week)

S M T W T F S

DAY FIVE

REVIEW AND DISCUSS

In what ways are you doing a good job at protecting your heart from "bad company"?

....

....

....

....

....

How do you usually respond when you have made a mistake and hurt someone?
Are you quick to apologize and make it right?

....

....

....

....

....

How have you seen God answer your prayers this week?

....

....

Scripture Writing Challenge

Rewrite:
"The Lord says, 'I will guide you along the best pathway for your life.
I will advise you and watch over you.' "
Psalm 32:8 (NLT)

....

....

....

....

Finishing Off

God, today I am feeling... (Circle or color)

 Happy
 Blessed
 Anxious
 Sad
 Angry

I feel this way because ....

....

Today I am thankful for ....

Today I am praying for ....

....

171

Go to page 189 and fill in your "Monthly Mood Tracker" chart.

Discussion Questions

• Week Three •

Pick one or more questions to discuss with your parents.

Kids ask your parents:

- Have you ever followed your heart and made a wrong choice?
- What does God want us to do when we make mistakes?
- This week I learned that bad company corrupts good character (1 Corinthians 15:33). What are some examples of bad company?

Parents ask your kids:

- How is God's Word similar to a compass?
- What did you learn about following your heart?
- What does it mean to "guard your heart?"

Family Prayer Requests:

....

....

....

....

Doodles

Use this empty space to draw or doodle!

Week Four
START AT THE CROSS
(How can I know Jesus more?)

Today is: (Color the day of the week)

S M T W T F S

DAY ONE

PLANTING A SEED

Start at the Cross
(How can I know Jesus more?)

"God saved you by his grace when you believed. And you can't take credit for this; it is a gift from God. Salvation is not a reward for the good things we have done, so none of us can boast about it."
Ephesians 2:8-9 (NLT)

Picture this: You and a group of your friends are outside in the baseball field hitting fly balls and enjoying what last bit of summer remains. Everyone is having a great time when you see your neighbor, Mr. Jones, come out of his front door and walk towards you.

"Hi kids," he smiles kindly. "I wondered if maybe you could move your game farther away from the street," he says. He points towards an obviously very expensive blue car just a couple yards away, "There are lots of cars close by."

You all agree and promise to move but as he turns his back and starts walking away you think to yourself, "Just one more hit and we'll move." Your bat cracks as it connects with the ball. It soars into the air as you watch the ball come down, suddenly you feel your heart sink. You hear a loud smash as it blows through the windshield of the nice blue car your neighbor pointed out to you only moments earlier.

You drop your bat and walk to the car with your heart in your throat. As you size up the damage your stomach flips in panic. You know without being told that the cost to repair the damage will be more than you could ever pay back on your own. What are you going to do? You glance behind you and see your neighbor frozen as he stares at you. It is clear that he saw everything.

In the Bible, God calls our unwillingness to obey Him, sin. We sin when we break God's law. Sometimes these sins can be easy to spot... cheating on a test or stealing something that doesn't belong to us. But other sins can be harder to spot: gossip, lying, unforgiveness towards someone, or wanting what someone else has. All of these things whether big or small are sin—and all of them affect our relationship with God. Like the broken windshield in our story, when we sin our relationship with God is damaged and a cost needs to be paid to repair it.

But what if the cost is too high that we are unable to pay? This week we will get to know Jesus and the cost He paid to repair our relationship with God.

176

Have you ever made a big mistake that you couldn't fix?
What happened? How did you feel?

....

....

....

....

....

....

....

....

Finishing Off

God, today I am feeling... (Circle or color)

Happy   **Blessed**   **Anxious**   **Sad**   **Angry**

I feel this way because ....

....

Today I am thankful for ....

Today I am praying for ....

....

Go to page 189 and fill in your "Monthly Mood Tracker" chart.

Today is: (Color the day of the week)

S   M   T   W   T   F   S

DAY TWO

WATERING FOR GROWTH

Yesterday we learned that our disobedience to God's Word is called sin. To know where our sin problem started we need to go all the way to the beginning, with Adam and Eve.

Read:

"The Lord God made all sorts of trees grow up from the ground-trees that were beautiful and that produced delicious fruit. In the middle of the garden he placed the tree of life and the tree of the knowledge of good and evil."

Genesis 2:9 (NLT)

and

"But the Lord God warned him, 'You may freely eat the fruit of every tree in the garden, except the tree of the knowledge of good and evil. If you eat its fruit, you are sure to die.' "

Genesis 2:16-17 (NLT)

God warned Adam and Eve not to eat from the fruit of one tree —the tree of knowing good and evil. Adam and Eve had an entire garden of fruit to eat from and only one was off limits. Have you ever been faced with the same rule? You can play anywhere in the house except the living room, or you can have any other snack before bedtime except the sugary one, or you can drink from any glass in the house except the expensive tea cup in your mom's china cabinet.

God had given Adam and Eve everything they needed. He had just one rule, not to eat of the tree of knowing good and evil. Did they listen?

Read:

"The serpent was the shrewdest of all the wild animals the Lord God had made. One day he asked the woman, 'Did God really say you must not eat the fruit from any of the trees in the garden?' 'Of course we may eat fruit from the trees in the garden,' the woman replied. 'It's only the fruit from the tree in the middle of the garden that we are not allowed to eat. God said, 'You must not eat it or even touch it; if you do, you will die.' 'You won't die!' the serpent replied to the woman. 'God knows that your eyes will be opened as soon as you eat it, and you will be like God, knowing both good and evil.' The woman was convinced. She saw that the tree was beautiful and its fruit looked delicious, and she wanted the wisdom it would give her. So she took some of the fruit and ate it. Then she gave some to her husband, who was with her, and he ate it, too."

Genesis 3:1-6 (NLT)

Uh oh. Adam and Even knew the right thing to do but they disobeyed. From that moment sin entered the world. Adam and Eve were forced to leave the garden and their relationship with God was damaged because of their sin.

Adam and Eve's sin had huge consequences for us even today. Tomorrow we will learn more about them.

178

Today I went to see the dentist for a checkup. He told me I needed braces on my top and bottom teeth for a whole year! A couple weeks later I went back and had them put on. They felt really funny and it was hard to talk at first. My dentist sent me home with a **no-no list** of things I couldn't eat until my braces came off. I can't believe that some of my most favorite things are on the "no-no" list! Popcorn, gum, suckers, taco chips, and even corn on the cob. It's not fair... this is going to be a long 12 months!

Have you ever wanted something more just because you were told you couldn't have it? Journal about it below.

....

....

....

Finishing Off

God, today I am feeling... (Circle or color)

Happy

Blessed

Anxious

Sad

Angry

I feel this way because ....

....

Today I am thankful for ....

Today I am praying for ....

....

179

Go to page 189 and fill in your "Monthly Mood Tracker" chart.

Today is: (Color the day of the week)

S M T W T F S

DAY THREE

GROWING ROOTS

Yesterday we learned about the very first sin. When Adam and Eve chose to disobey God's command to not touch or eat the fruit from the tree of knowing good and evil, they sinned. When we disobey God's Word we sin too.

Have you ever thought, "But I am a good person. I don't steal or say bad words. I do my homework and try my best to obey my parents. Is that what God wants from me? He wants me to be really good?"

Read:

"As the Scriptures say, 'No one is righteous—not even one.' "
Romans 3:10 (NLT)

Underline the word **righteous**.
The definition of righteous is "innocent or without fault or guilt."
God's standard is much higher than just being good. His standard is perfect innocence.

Read:

"For everyone has sinned; we all fall short of God's glorious standard."
Romans 3:23 (NLT)

Underline the word **everyone**.
According to this verse is anyone perfectly innocent of sin?

Yes   No

Adam and Eve's decision brought sin into the world. The Bible says that there is not one person who does not sin.

Imagine sin as a germ that we are born with. No amount of medicine or effort on our part can get rid of it. When we are selfish, lash out in anger, are jealous, or disobedient to our parents we are displaying symptoms of our sin.

No matter how hard we try we will never be able to live a perfect, sinless life. We cannot fix our sin issue by being good, we need a master physician.

God knew when He created us that we were never going to measure up to perfection. God loved us so much that He wanted us in Heaven with Him for eternity. God knew that we needed a rescue plan.

Tomorrow we will learn about God's solution to our sin problem.

180

If sin were a germ what do you think it would look like? Doodle and color it in the magnifying glass.

Finishing Off

God, today I am feeling... (Circle or color)

Happy

Blessed

Anxious

Sad

Angry

I feel this way because ....
....

Today I am thankful for ....

Today I am praying for ....

....

Go to page 189 and fill in your "Monthly Mood Tracker" chart.

WEEK FOUR
Start at the Cross

DAY FOUR
HARVESTING THE FRUIT

Yesterday we learned that we all make mistakes. It is really important to understand that making mistakes is a part of being human. No matter how hard we try we will never be perfect. It can be really discouraging to realize that we will always struggle with making good choices. Our sin is a part of us and there is nothing that we can do to change that.

But the Bible tells us that there is still hope for us:

Read:

"He himself is the sacrifice that atones for our sins-and not only our sins but the sins of all the world."

1 John 2:2 (NLT)

Circle the word **atones**. The word "atone" means to make right an offense. Think of the boy in our story from day one, his mistake cost him. The damage was done to the car and someone needed to pay and the price was far greater than the boy could ever pay. The Bible says that every sin we make has a cost to it. God knew that there was no way people could pay for every single sin they would ever commit so He paid the price of the entire world's sin, in one payment—Jesus.

Read:

"He personally carried our sins in his body on the cross so that we can be dead to sin and live for what is right. By his wounds you are healed."

1 Peter 2:24 (NLT)

Circle the word **healed**.

Yesterday we thought about sin as a germ we are born with. No amount of medicine or effort on our part can get rid of it. We need a master physician to heal us.

Jesus is the master physician. 1 John 2:2 says that Jesus paid the price for every sin we have ever made or will ever make. His healing is a gift to us that cost Him His life. Not because we earned it or deserve it but because He loves us.

Read:

"that if you confess with your mouth Jesus as Lord, and believe in your heart that God raised Him from the dead, you will be saved."

Romans 10:9 (NASB)

To confess means to tell God that you know you cannot pay for your own sins, the price is too high. Romans 10:9 says that if we believe that God raised Jesus from the dead and admit that we need His forgiveness then we will be forgiven. Have you done that yet? If not, use the prayer on the next page.

182

Dear God,
I know that I have made many mistakes. No matter how hard I try, I can't be perfect. I believe that Jesus died on the cross to pay for my sins. Thank you for loving me that much. Please forgive me for the times that I don't made good choices. Please forgive my sin and come live in my heart.

In Jesus' name, Amen.

If you prayed the prayer above, congratulations! The Bible promises that because of your confession and Jesus' death on the cross you can know without a doubt that every sin you have ever made and will ever make is forgiven. The angels in Heaven are celebrating!

Now make sure you share this great news with someone!

Finishing Off

God, today I am feeling... (Circle or color)

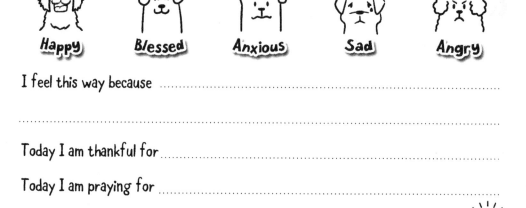

Happy   Blessed   Anxious   Sad   Angry

I feel this way because ....

....

Today I am thankful for ....

Today I am praying for ....

....

Go to page 189 and fill in your "Monthly Mood Tracker" chart.

WEEK FOUR
Start at the Cross

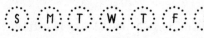

DAY FIVE
REVIEW AND DISCUSS

This week you learned that every one sins. According to what we learned, why is being "good" not enough?

....

....

....

....

....

....

As we wrap up our study time together, think back to everything you have learned over the last 3 months. What has really stuck out to you?

....

....

....

....

....

....

....

....

....

....

184 ....

Scripture Writing Challenge

Rewrite:
"that if you confess with your mouth Jesus as Lord, and believe in your heart that God raised Him from the dead, you will be saved."

Romans 10:9 (NASB)

....

....

....

....

Finishing Off

God, today I am feeling... (Circle or color)

Happy

Blessed

Anxious

Sad

Angry

I feel this way because ....

....

Today I am thankful for ....

Today I am praying for ....

....

185

Go to page 189 and fill in your "Monthly Mood Tracker" chart.

Discussion Questions

• Week Four •

Pick one or more questions to discuss with your parents.

Kids ask your parents:

- Describe one mistake you have made that you wish you could take back.
- What is one thing you want me to know when I mess up?
- Describe a time when you were thankful for God's forgiveness.
- How have you seen me grow over the last 3 months?

Parents ask your kids:

- What happened in the story about the boy and the windshield?
- Do you understand that our sin is too expensive for us to pay for on our own?
- What is your favorite lesson you have learned over the last 3 months?
- How have you seen God answer your prayers over the last 3 months?

Family Prayer Requests:

....

....

....

....

Doodles

Use this empty space to draw or doodle!

MONTHLY MOOD
TRACKER
CHAPTER THREE

Color a dot under how you are feeling today.

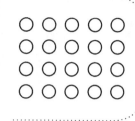

Angry

Sad

Anxious

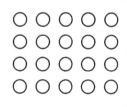

Blessed

Happy

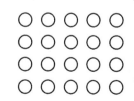

Notes

Notes

Notes

Notes

Notes

Notes

Notes

Notes

Notes

Notes

Notes

Notes

Printed in Great Britain
by Amazon

42501424R00116